T0148738

CONSTITUTIONAL CONSERVATISM

HOOVER
INSTITUTION

STANFORD
UNIVERSITY

*The Hoover Institution gratefully acknowledges
the following individuals and foundations
for their significant support of the*
BOYD AND JILL SMITH TASK FORCE ON
VIRTUES OF A FREE SOCIETY

Boyd and Jill Smith
William E. Simon Foundation

BOYD AND JILL SMITH TASK FORCE ON VIRTUES OF A FREE SOCIETY

CONSTITUTIONAL CONSERVATISM

Liberty, Self-Government, and Political Moderation

Peter Berkowitz

HOOVER INSTITUTION PRESS

Stanford University   *Stanford, California*

www.hoover.org

Hoover Institution Press Publication No. 634

Hoover Institution at Leland Stanford Junior University, Stanford, California, 94305-6010

First printing 2013
20 19 18 17 16 15 14 13   9 8 7 6 5 4 3 2

Manufactured in the United States of America

The paper used in this publication meets the minimum Requirements of the American National Standard for Information Sciences—Permanence of Paper for Printed Library Materials, ANSI/NISO Z39.48-1992. ∞

Library of Congress Cataloging-in-Publication Data

Berkowitz, Peter, 1959–   author.
Constitutional conservatism : Liberty, self-government, and political moderation / Peter Berkowitz.
     pages   cm. — (Hoover Institution Press publication ; no. 634)
Includes bibliographical references and index.
ISBN 978-0-8179-1604-6 (cloth : alk. paper) —
ISBN 978-0-8179-1606-0 (ebook)
1. Constitutional law—United States.   2. Conservatism—United States.
3. Liberty.   4. United States—Politics and government.
I. Title.   II. Series: Hoover Institution Press publication ; 634.

KF4550.B385   2013
320.520973—dc23   2012045831

Contents

Preface

In late October 2008, over breakfast at the Stanford Park Hotel, Hoover Institution Deputy Director David Brady criticized social conservatives' hold on the Republican Party. With the economic crisis deepening and Democratic presidential nominee Senator Barack Obama poised for a historic victory, it was time, Brady declared, for libertarians, or limited-government conservatives, to break ranks and go their own way. I replied that many social conservatives seemed to have reached the same conclusion about the need to part company with libertarians. Then I asked Brady, one of the nation's leading experts on American electoral politics, whether either of the two main camps within American conservatism was capable of forming a governing majority without the other. Propriety prevents me from reproducing Professor Brady's colorful reply. Nevertheless, today, as in 2008, neither social conservatives nor libertarians can form a governing majority alone.

But can social conservatives and libertarians ever move beyond a *modus vivendi?* Is a meeting of minds possible? Can those who emphasize safeguarding traditional morality and religion and those who stress the need to keep government firmly within fixed bounds form a principled alliance?

In January 2009, in an op-ed in *The Wall Street Journal,* and the next month in a long essay in *Policy Review,* I sought to identify the political principles social conservatives and libertarians share, or should share, and to sketch the common ground on which they could and should join forces.[1] This book develops the argument outlined in those articles: the top political priority for both social conservatives and limited-government conservatives should be to conserve the principles of liberty embodied in the American Constitution and to pursue reform in light of them.[2]

---

1. See "Conservatives Can Unite Around the Constitution," *The Wall Street Journal,* Jan. 2, 2009, available at http://online.wsj.com/article/SB123086011 787848029.html; and "Constitutional Conservatism," *Policy Review,* Feb./ Mar. 2009, available at http://www.hoover.org/publications/policy-review /article/5580.

2. This book also freely draws upon several articles in which I have grappled with challenges involved in conserving and correcting liberty: "Burke's Words Should Hearten Dismayed Conservatives," *Real Clear Politics,* Feb. 25, 2012, available at http://www.realclearpolitics.com/articles/2012/02/25/burkes_ words_should_hearten_dismayed_conservatives_113248.html; "God and Man at Yale Turns 60," *Real Clear Politics,* Nov. 5, 2011, available at http://www. realclearpolitics.com/articles/2011/11/05/god_and_man_at_yale_ turns_60_111964.html; "The Myth of Conservative Purity," *The Wall Street Journal,* Sept. 7, 2011, available at http://www.hoover.org/news/daily-report /91897; "Truman, Reagan, and Bush Were Right," PJ Media, Feb. 23, 2011, available at http://pjmedia.com/blog/truman-reagan-and-bush-were-right; "What Would a Return to the Constitution Entail?," PJ Media, Jan. 7, 2011, available at http://pjmedia.com/blog/what-would-a-return-to-the-constitution -entail; "The Cheshire Cat Conservative," *Policy Review,* Oct./Nov. 2010 (a review of William F. Buckley Jr., *Athwart History: Half a Century of Polemics, Animadversions, and Illuminations: A William F. Buckley Jr. Omnibus,* eds. Linda Bridges and Roger Kimball), available at http://www.hoover.org/publications/ policy-review/article/49871; "The Death of Conservatism Was Greatly Exaggerated," *The Wall Street Journal,* Aug. 28, 2010, available at http://online.wsj .com/article/SB10001424052748704147804575455090270186082.html; "Reagan's Candid Way," *Policy Review,* Oct./Nov. 2009 (a review of Steven F. Hayward, *The Age of Reagan: The Conservative Counterrevolution 1980–1989*), available at http://www.hoover.org/publications/policy-review/article/5436.

A constitutional conservatism, I continue to contend, can be principled and politically potent.

As Barack Obama's star rose in 2008, it became fashionable among leading progressive journalists to proclaim the death of conservatism. In late October 2008, *New Yorker* staff writer George Packer reported "the complete collapse of the four-decade project that brought conservatism to power in America."[3] Two weeks later, the day after Obama's election, *Washington Post* columnist E.J. Dionne proclaimed "the end of a conservative era" that had begun with the rise of Ronald Reagan.[4] And in February 2009, shortly after President Obama's inauguration, *New York Times* Book Review and Week in Review editor Sam Tanenhaus, writing in *The New Republic,* declared that "movement conservatism is exhausted and quite possibly dead."[5] Tanenhaus even purported to discern in Obama "the emergence of a president who seems more thoroughly steeped in the principles of Burkean conservatism than any significant thinker or political figure on the right."[6]

In heralding conservatism's death, these pundits underestimated the unpredictability in human affairs that the conservative tradition rightly emphasizes. They also conflated the flagging fortunes of George W. Bush's Republican Party with conservatism's popular appeal. And they failed to grasp the variety of imperatives

---

3. "End of an Era," *The New Yorker,* Oct. 23, 2008, available at http://www .newyorker.com/online/blogs/georgepacker/2008/10/step-back-a-mom.html.

4. "A New Era for America," *The Washington Post,* Nov. 5, 2008, available at http://www.washingtonpost.com/wp-dyn/content/article/2008/11/04 /AR2008110404476.html.

5. "Conservatism Is Dead," *The New Republic,* Feb. 18, 2009, available at http://www.tnr.com/article/politics/conservatism-dead.

6. Ibid.

that flow from conservative principles in America, and the full range of tasks connected to preserving freedom.

The left was not alone in supposing that Obama's 2008 victory marked the demise of American conservatism. As President Obama settled into the White House four years ago, more than a few on the right feared that conservatism had been gravely wounded and was destined to wander for decades in the political wilderness.

By summer 2009, however, a Tea Party–sparked conservative revival was well underway.[7] A decentralized grassroots movement dedicated to limited constitutional government and fiscal discipline, the Tea Party counted among its membership a substantial number of social conservatives. Tea Party members were responding in no small measure to President Obama's most un-Burkean attempt to enact a transformative progressive agenda—in opposition to majority sentiment and contrary to Obama's efforts on the campaign trail, facilitated by a fawning press, to paint himself as moderate, pragmatic, and post-partisan.

In the November 2010 midterm elections, the Tea Party's energy and engagement contributed to a historic swing toward the GOP. Though declared down for the count only two years before, Republicans not only took the United States House of Representatives by a comfortable margin and achieved near parity in the Senate, but also recorded dramatic gains in state Houses throughout the country. As I write these words, conservatives are once again taking stock after the loss of a close presidential election

---

7. Thus was Tanenhaus's book, *The Death of Conservatism* (New York: Random House, 2009), which appeared barely half a year after his article, refuted by events months before its September 2009 publication. See my review of Tanenhaus's book, "An Exaggerated Death," *National Review Online,* Sept. 3, 2009, available at http://www.nationalreview.com/articles/228168/exaggerated-death/peter-berkowitz.

that was very much within their power to win. Now more than ever, clarity about constitutional conservatism is essential.

Since 2009, the term constitutional conservatism has increasingly come into vogue. Sarah Palin touted it, Tea Party members embraced it, and *National Affairs* editor Yuval Levin wrote a penetrating essay expounding it.[8] Notwithstanding differences of opinion about its precise meaning, constitutional conservatism captures the notion that renewing American conservatism depends on reclaiming the principles of liberty embodied in America's founding charter of government.

Among the Constitution's most remarkable features is its institutionalization of political moderation. I do not mean that conniving and cowardly offspring of expedience and ambition that betrays principle to get ahead or just get along. I refer instead to political moderation well understood, which accommodates, balances, and calibrates to translate rival and worthy principles into practice. The Constitution weaves political moderation well understood into the very structure of self-government. It does this out of a sober recognition of the imperfections of human nature, the importance but scarcity of virtue, and the need to limit government to secure freedom. The central aim of this book is to recover the constitutional connection between liberty, self-government, and political moderation.

I do not seek to mediate quarrels among scholars about the history of ideas, as valuable as that service can be, or to elaborate concrete public policy proposals, as urgent as that task is. Rather,

---

8. Sarah Palin, *America by Heart: Reflections on Family, Faith, and Flag* (New York: Harper, 2011), pp. 266–267; Constitutional Conservatives Fund, available at http://fundconservatives.com/tags/mike-lee; Yuval Levin, "What Is Constitutional Conservatism?," *National Review,* Nov. 28, 2011, available at http://www.nationalreview.com/articles/283326/what-constitutional-conservatism-yuval-levin.

I distill the principles of freedom inscribed in a tradition of thinking that stretches from eighteenth-century British statesman Edmund Burke's extraordinary defense of liberty through *The Federalist*'s authoritative case for the Constitution during the ratification debates of 1787 and 1788 to the rebirth of conservatism in post–World War II America. At each of these critical moments, the conservative tradition—or rather the conservative side of the larger liberal tradition that goes back at least to John Locke's grounding of legitimate political power in the natural freedom and equality of all human beings in *Two Treatises of Government* (1689)—has been distinguished by its understanding that liberty and the limited government that secures it depend on tradition, order, and virtue. Constitutional conservatism well understood seeks to revivify that understanding.

Washington, D.C.
November 2012

CHAPTER 1

Seizing the Moment,
Renewing the Legacy

To make a government requires no great prudence. Settle the seat of power, teach obedience, and the work is done. To give freedom is still more easy. It is not necessary to guide; it only requires to let go the rein. But to form a *free government*, that is, to temper together these opposite elements of liberty and restraint in one consistent work, requires much thought, deep reflection, a sagacious, powerful, and combining mind.

—Edmund Burke, *Reflections on the Revolution in France*

After their dismal performance in the 2008 election, conservatives had reason for gloom. They also had reason to take heart. After all, the election showed that the American constitutional order was working as designed. The Constitution presupposes a responsive electorate, and respond the electorate did: to a spendthrift and feckless Republican Congress; to a stalwart but frequently ineffectual Republican president; and to a Republican presidential candidate who—for all his mastery of foreign affairs, extensive Washington experience, and honorable public service—proved incapable of crafting a coherent and compelling message.

Both the election of Barack Obama as president and the electorate's response to the conduct of the Obama administration in office provided further reason to appreciate our constitutional order's vitality. Americans left and right justly took pride in

President Obama's historic victory. His emergence from obscure origins to become the first African American to occupy the nation's highest office testified to abundant opportunity in America. Entering office in late January 2009 with a 68 percent approval rating, President Obama embodied a stunning refutation of the calumny promulgated by many progressive intellectuals. As late as spring 2008, some continued to declare in private and to whisper in public that their fellow citizens were too racist to elect a black man president.

But politics, certainly the politics of liberal democracy in America, does not stand still. In late 2009 and early 2010, the people of three states whose electoral votes went to candidate Obama in 2008 delivered a reproach to President Obama's administration, particularly its dramatic increases in government spending, its projected massive enlargement of the annual deficit and the national debt, and its plans for a sweeping overhaul of health care. In gubernatorial contests in November 2009, Virginia elected Republican Bob McDonnell and New Jersey elected Republican Chris Christie. A few months later, in Massachusetts' January 2010 special election, Republican Scott Brown won the Senate seat that Democratic icon Edward M. Kennedy held for forty-seven years. On the campaign trail, Brown had vigorously opposed the president's signature health care legislation.

Democrats defied the voters' message. In March 2010, despite polls showing opposition by a majority of the public, Congressional Democrats proceeded to narrowly pass broad health care reform legislation on a strict party line vote and by means of an obscure procedural maneuver. President Obama promptly and triumphantly signed into law the Affordable Care Act.

Well before the end of Obama's first year in office, many independents—who voted for him in significant numbers—began to feel deceived by the far-reaching progressive agenda the president had unveiled once safely ensconced in the White House. To be sure, Senator Obama's campaign mantra of hope and change signaled large, if vague, ambition, and in the campaign's homestretch he told an adoring crowd, "We are five days away from fundamentally transforming the United States of America."[1] Yet candidate Obama also cultivated the image of a moderate in style and substance, a pragmatist and problem-solver, a prudent steward of the country's finances, and a leader who aspired to reach out across the aisle and represent conservative voices and outlooks, too.[2] President Obama's tenacious pursuit of costly and comprehensive health care reform throughout 2009, despite a severely weakened economy, and into 2010, against the wishes of an increasingly mobilized electorate, dramatized the priority he gave to progressive transformation.[3]

This is not what independents who voted for Obama in 2008 bargained for, to say nothing of conservatives who voted for McCain. Those who opposed President Obama's transformative agenda argued, organized, held town-hall meetings, and rallied. In the momentous November 2010 midterm elections, they gave Republicans a substantial majority in the House and significantly narrowed the gap with the majority Democrats in the Senate, effectively providing Congressional conservatives the power to

---

1. "Thousands Cheer Obama at Rally for Change," *The Missourian*, Oct. 28, 2008, available at http://www.columbiamissourian.com/stories/2008/10/30/obama-speaks-crowd-40000.

2. See Cass Sunstein, "The Empiricist Strikes Back," *The New Republic*, Sept. 10, 2008; and Sunstein, "The Visionary Minimalist," *The New Republic*, Jan. 30, 2008.

3. For an analysis of progressivism's anti-democratic and illiberal tendencies—both the original progressivism and Obama's new progressivism—see Peter Berkowitz, "Obama and the State of Progressivism, 2011," *Policy Review*, Dec. 2010/Jan. 2011, available at http://www.hoover.org/publications/policy-review/article/57971.

check much of the president's progressive policy making. A year and a half later, in June 2012, the voters of Wisconsin rejected the public union–led effort to recall Republican Governor Scott Walker, who had made good on his campaign promise to rein in public unions by curbing their collective bargaining rights and compelling them to pay a larger share toward their health care insurance and retirement benefits. In November 2012, however, President Obama gained a narrow victory over Mitt Romney, even as Republicans successfully returned a sizable blocking majority to the House of Representatives and achieved historic majorities both in governorships and in state legislatures.

Needless to say, conservatives too have been guilty of overreach, reflected in a proclivity to believe that what was most needed was greater purity in conservative ranks. Following Obama's 2008 victory and a major loss of Republican seats in that year's Congressional elections, some social conservatives pointed to successful ballot initiatives in Arizona, California, and Florida that rejected same-sex marriage as evidence that the country had remained socially conservative, and that deviation from the social conservative agenda accounted for GOP electoral setbacks. The purists, however, conveniently overlooked the trend lines. In California's 2000 ballot initiative, 61 percent of voters rejected same-sex marriage, but in 2008, opposition in the nation's most populous state fell to 52 percent. Notwithstanding North Carolina's decision in 2012 to restrict marriage to heterosexual couples, the data show that the public is steadily growing more accepting of same-sex marriage: national polls indicate that opposition, including that of conservatives, is strongest among older voters and declines as voters' age decreases. In November 2012, voters in Maine, Maryland, and Washington became the first to legalize same sex marriage through state-wide elections.

Meanwhile, by the end of George W. Bush's second term, many libertarians had grown disgusted by Republican profligacy.

They were discomfited by, or downright opposed to, the Bush administration's support for a constitutional amendment banning same-sex marriage. They also disliked the Bush administration's continuation of the moratorium on government funding of embryonic stem cell research, which had been in place in one form or another almost continuously since the Reagan administration. And they were angered by the intensive Republican-led intervention by the federal government in 2005 to prevent Terri Schiavo's husband from lawfully removing the feeding tubes that for 15 years had kept his wife alive in a persistent vegetative state. Some of these libertarians went so far as to entertain dreams of repudiating social conservatives and forming a coalition with moderate Democrats. That dream was quickly dashed by President Obama's big-spending ways.

The purists in both camps ignored simple electoral math. Slice and dice citizens' opinions and voting patterns in the fifty states as you like, neither social conservatives nor libertarians can fashion a majority without the aid of the other.

Nevertheless, the quest for purity resurfaced in the 2012 Republican primaries. At one time or another, and sometimes as a group, Tim Pawlenty, Ron Paul, Michelle Bachman, Rick Perry, Herman Cain, Rick Santorum, Newt Gingrich, and their supporters denounced Mitt Romney for a variety of conservative impurities. In part, the raucous campaign for the GOP nomination reflected the ordinary rough and tumble of democratic politics. In part it reflected Romney's struggle to clarify his positions and define his agenda. And in part it presented the embarrassing spectacle of Republican hopefuls and their enthusiasts forming a circular firing squad with the party's leading contender in the middle. Underlying the excesses was a failure to grasp principle, or rather to grasp that conservatism in America comprises a family of rival and worthy principles that require accommodation—

to each other, to the exigencies of the moment, and to the changing habits and opinions of the American people.

Understanding this family of principles is critical to grasping why social conservatives, libertarians, and the neoconservatives who are also crucial to conservative electoral hopes and political fortunes, do not merely form a coalition of convenience. Because the principles are inscribed in the American Constitution and the political theory that underlies it, the task of conserving them deserves the name constitutional conservatism.

Constitutional conservatism well understood puts liberty first and teaches that political moderation is indispensable to securing, preserving, and extending liberty's blessings. The American Constitution it seeks to conserve presupposes natural freedom and equality. It draws legitimacy both from democratic consent and from the protection of individual rights—particularly those of religion, speech, assembly, and property. It limits and enumerates government's powers while furnishing government with the incentives and tools to discharge its responsibilities effectively. It reflects and refines popular will through a complex scheme of representation. It provides checks and balances by dispersing and blending power among three distinct branches of the federal government, as well as among the federal and state governments. It assumes the primacy of self-interest but also the capacity of and necessity for citizens to rise above it through the exercise of virtue. It welcomes a diverse array of voluntary associations because they are an expression of liberty, to prevent any one from dominating, and because they serve as schools for the virtues of freedom. And it recognizes the special role of families and religious faith in cultivating these virtues.

Constitutional conservatism belongs to a distinguished tradition of defending liberty. It finds instruction and inspiration in the eighteenth-century speeches and writings of British statesman Edmund Burke, who is regarded as the father of modern conservatism, though it would be more accurate to describe him as the father of that form of modern conservatism devoted to the conservation and correction of liberty. It is embedded in the American Constitution and flows out of the ideas elaborated most compellingly in *The Federalist,* the masterpiece of American political thought the immediate purpose of which was to persuade New York voters in 1787 and 1788 to ratify the Constitution, and whose persuasive force stemmed in significant measure from the quality of its reasoning about the enduring principles of self-government. And constitutional conservatism is exhibited in the high points of the post–World War II renewal of conservatism in America, including the writings of eminent public intellectuals such as Friedrich A. Hayek, Milton Friedman, Russell Kirk, Whittaker Chambers, William F. Buckley Jr., Frank S. Meyer, and Irving Kristol, and in the speeches and actions of such seminal political figures as Barry Goldwater, Ronald Reagan, Newt Gingrich, and George W. Bush.

When applied in the spirit of political moderation out of which they arose, the principles of constitutional conservatism are crucial to the restoration of an electorally enduring and politically responsible conservatism. As in all large families and vibrant traditions, clashes over priorities and policies will persist. Yet rallying around the principles of liberty on which the nation was founded is the best means over the long term to conserve the political conditions hospitable to traditional morality and religious faith. It is also the best means over the long term to conserve the political conditions that promote free markets and the prosperity and opportunity free markets bring. And a constitutional conservatism provides a sturdy framework for developing a distinctive reform agenda to confront today's challenges—an agenda that both social conservatives and limited government conservatives, consistent with their highest hopes, can and should embrace.

CHAPTER 2

Burke:

The Conservation and Correction of Liberty

Feuding among American conservatives for the title True Conservative is nothing new. Ever since conservatism in America crystallized as a recognizable school in the 1950s, more than a few libertarians and more than a few social conservatives— and their forebears, traditionalist conservatives—have wanted to flee from or banish the other. To be sure, the passion for purity in politics is perennial. But the tension between liberty and tradition inscribed in modern conservatism has exacerbated the stress and strain in the contending conservative camps. Fortunately, a lesson of political moderation is also inscribed in the modern conservative tradition, and nowhere more durably or compellingly than at its beginning.

Moderating the tension between liberty, or doing as you please, and tradition, or doing as has been done in the past, is a hallmark of the speeches and writings of eighteenth-century British statesman Edmund Burke. While the conservative spirit is enduring and while some have always been more amply endowed with the inclination to preserve inherited ways and others more moved by the impulse to improve or supersede them, the distinctively modern form of conservatism emerged with Burke's 1790 polemic, *Reflections on the Revolution in France*. Writing as a friend of liberty and enlightenment, Burke eloquently exposed the brutality of the revolutionaries' determination, inspired by a perverse understanding of liberty and enlightenment, to transform political life by upending and sweeping away tradition, custom, and the inherited moral order. Burke's conservatism operates within the broad contours of the larger liberal tradition and embraces much of the spirit of the eighteenth-century Enlightenment. It is distinguished by its determination to moderate the tendencies toward excess that mark both liberty and reason.

Burke's devotion to "a spirit of rational liberty"[1] drives the great reform efforts of his political career: conciliation with America, toleration for Ireland's Catholics, and protection of the interests and rights of the people of India. But even if we had only the *Reflections,* he would still deserve to be counted among our preeminent teachers concerning the balance of principles that favors liberty.

The causes to which Burke dedicated himself, and the well-wrought arguments he summoned in their behalf, teach that the paramount political task is to defend liberty. They also illustrate that while the purpose of politics is not to perfect man, securing the rights shared equally by all depends on tradition, religion, and community cultivating the virtues that fit citizens for freedom. And they clarify how the rival interests, multiplicity of groups and associations, and competing conceptions of happiness that characterize free societies make accommodation, balance, and calibration indispensable to the conservative mission. Burke's storied career demonstrates that political moderation is not only consistent with but essential to vindicating the principles of liberty.

---

1. Edmund Burke, *Reflections on the Revolution in France,* in *The Works of the Right Honourable Edmund Burke,* Vol. III (London: John C. Nimmo, 1887), p. 235, available at http://www.gutenberg.org/files/15679/15679-h/15679-h .htm#REFLECTIONS.

Liberty and the French Revolution

Burke's *Reflections on the Revolution in France* is the work of a Whig who cherished freedom and, in the name of individual liberty, sought throughout his long parliamentary career, in battles with the Tories as well as with fellow Whigs, to limit the political power of throne and altar. But to limit is not to abolish, and can be consistent with cherishing, as it was in Burke's case. He saw that within proper boundaries, religious faith disciplined and elevated hearts and minds, and monarchy upheld the continuity of tradition, reflected the benefits of hierarchy and order, and provided energy and agility in government. Both institutions, in his assessment, encouraged virtues crucial to liberty's preservation.

Whereas for the sake of liberty Burke sought to limit the political power of the monarchy in Great Britain, he defended the throne of Louis XVI in France against what he regarded as the revolutionaries' radical conception of freedom. Burke warned that the French Revolution presented "a great crisis, not of the affairs of France alone, but of all Europe, perhaps of more than Europe."[2] Indeed, he contended that "all circumstances taken together, the French Revolution is the most astonishing that has hitherto happened in the world."[3] The crux of the matter was that the revolutionaries' novel doctrine demanded more than a change of government; it required "a total revolution,"[4] one that would break from and cast aside established beliefs, practices, and institutions.

---

2. *Reflections on the Revolution in France*, p. 243.
3. Ibid., pp. 243–244.
4. Ibid., p. 370. See also Edmund Burke, "Letter to a Noble Lord," *The Works of the Right Honourable Edmund Burke*, Vol. V (London: John C. Nimmo, 1887), pp. 175, 197, available at http://www.gutenberg.org/files/15701 /15701-h/15701-h.htm#ATTACKS_MADE_UPON_MR_BURKE.

In contrast, Burke championed "a manly, moral, regulated liberty."[5] Liberty well understood, he argued, appreciates the power of self-interest but stresses self-restraint.[6] It values calculation, planning, and ambitious state undertakings but attaches great significance to the steady development over centuries of sentiments, manners, and morals.[7] Such liberty depends on a science of government—of constructing, conserving, and reforming the state—that involves "a deep knowledge of human nature and human necessities, and of the things which facilitate or obstruct the various ends which are to be pursued by the mechanism of civil institutions."[8] It recognizes that "the little platoon we belong to in society"—family, religious community, village or town—is the original source of "public affections" and serves as a school in which we develop "a love to our country and to mankind."[9] It rejects theoreticians' and intellectuals' definition of "the rights of men," which legitimate license without limits. Instead, liberty well understood affirms "the *real* rights of men," grounded in the advantages for which civil society is formed, including the right to live under the rule of law; to own and acquire property and to pass it on to one's children; and generally to live with one's family as one sees fit provided one does not trespass on the rights of others.[10] The primary aim of government, which Burke characterized as "a contrivance of human wisdom to provide for human *wants*," is to secure these rights.[11] Just where the exercise of freedom passes over into a violation of another's rights and how best to use one's

5. *Reflections on the Revolution in France,* p. 240.
6. Ibid., p. 310.
7. Ibid., pp. 331–336.
8. Ibid., p. 311.
9. Ibid., p. 292.
10. Ibid., pp. 308–309.
11. Ibid., p. 310.

freedom to live well could only be determined by prudent reflection on tradition and custom, because they embodied the nation's accumulated wisdom concerning the organization and conduct of human affairs.

Prudence, Burke famously observed, is "the god of this lower world."[12] It carefully considers circumstances, which "give in reality to every political principle its distinguishing color and discriminating effect," and which "render every civil and political scheme beneficial or noxious to mankind."[13] Prudence serves political moderation by mediating between principle and practice. It guides the reconciliation of liberty with the requirements of tradition, order, and virtue by taking the measure of all and, to the extent possible in the fluid and murky world of politics, issuing in judgments and actions that give each its due.

According to Burke, the French revolutionaries were immoderate in the extreme. By overthrowing monarchy and religion, they aimed to achieve emancipation from not merely a specific tradition or custom but the very authority of tradition and custom. Their goal, unreasonable in the extreme, was to establish an empire built on abstract reason alone. Prudent application of principle to circumstance would be unnecessary. Instead, they would mold circumstances to comply with pure reason's demands. Marching under the banner of "the rights of man," they set out to deduce the structure of a society of free and equal citizens without regard to the beliefs and practices, the passions and interests, the attachments and associations that fashion character and form conduct.

---

12. Edmund Burke, "Letter to the Sheriffs of the City of Bristol, on the Affairs of America," *The Works of the Right Honourable Edmund Burke*, Vol. II (London: John C. Nimmo, 1887), p. 226, available at http://www.gutenberg.org/files/15198/15198-h/15198-h.htm#SHERIFFS_OF_THE_CITY_OF_BRISTOL.

13. *Reflections on the Revolution in France,* pp. 239–240.

Rather than counting on education grounded in history, literature, and the sciences to discipline and elevate a recalcitrant human nature, the revolutionaries sought to remake human nature and society to fit reason's supposed revelations about citizens' true wants and needs, rights, and obligations. The realization of the revolutionaries' ambitions, Burke immediately discerned, would depend on the ruthless resort to violence. Anticipating not only Robespierre and the Reign of Terror but twentieth-century totalitarianism, Burke presciently argued that the determination to use the power of the state to create a new humanity would bring about the dehumanization of man.

The quarrel between Burke and the French revolutionaries comes down not to whether liberty is good or is even the leading purpose of politics—Burke thought it was both—but to the material and moral conditions and the political institutions most conducive to securing, preserving, and extending it. The French revolutionaries put their faith in government's ability to set the people free by developing institutions that satisfy citizens' sensibilities by aggressively transforming them. In contrast, Burke emphasized the moral and political benefits that flow to liberty from the time-tested beliefs, practices, and institutions beyond government's immediate purview that structure social life and cultivate manners and morals. The progressive side of the liberal tradition, the roots of which extend back to the French Revolution, tends to see traditional understandings of order and virtue as obstacles to freedom. In contrast, the conservative side of the liberal tradition, in the spirit of Burke, sees in them pillars of freedom and seeks to conserve the nongovernmental institutions—the family, religious faith, the voluntary associations of civil society—that sustain them.

Notwithstanding the veneration of the past and the excoriation of revolutionary innovation to which he gave expression in the *Reflections*, Burke was no reactionary who dogmatically clung to the old and rejected the new. He observed in the *Reflections* that because circumstances are constantly changing, "a state without the means of some change is without the means of its conservation."[14] Of course, the change in question must be prudent, wisely adapting enduring principles to the ordinary vicissitudes of politics. In extraordinary times, states must adjust to substantial shifts in circumstances, sentiment, and practice.

Prudent change depends on combining and reconciling "the two principles of conservation and correction."[15] The balancing of a conserving that is mindful of the need to correct and a correcting that proceeds with an eye to what deserves to be conserved is, in a free society, not an unwelcome political necessity. Such prudence is inseparable from respect for tradition and custom, because tradition and custom typically present not a clear-cut path but a "choice of inheritance."[16] Since the right choice about tradition must be freely and reasonably made, and since the reasonable use of freedom depends on the virtues nourished by tradition, liberty and tradition are mutually dependent.

This mutual dependence provides an opening to moderate the claims of liberty and tradition which, in a free society, frequently pull in opposing directions. To justly moderate, or harmonize, the competing claims of liberty and tradition, one must respect necessity without thoughtlessly acquiescing to what only appears necessary, and compromise on behalf of principle rather than compromise principle. Thus political moderation should not be confused with the absence of strong passion. It requires restraining the desire to vindicate immediately and completely a single principle

---

14. Ibid., p. 259.
15. Ibid.
16. Ibid., p. 275.

and instead working to vindicate the whole family of rival and worthy principles on which the conservation and correction of liberty depends. As Burke's career as a reformer vividly demonstrates, political moderation is propelled by a passion to strike the most reasonable balance among worthy but incomplete ends for the sake of liberty. Political moderation is a crucial part of the government of the self on which self-government in a free society depends.

Liberty and Reform

The need for prudent reform to meet the changing requirements of liberty was the dominant theme of Burke's nearly thirty-year political career in Great Britain's Parliament in the late 1700s. Britain then governed the largest empire the world had ever seen. The empire was distinguished not only by its reach but by the principle of liberty in which it was rooted. Burke believed that to conserve the empire, Britain had to recognize the convergence between its obligation to respect liberty and its interest in doing so—a convergence that held not only at home but in all its far-flung possessions and undertakings. Even when it meant differing from his constituents—and in his greatest moments Burke championed causes that many of his constituents strongly opposed—he ardently defended liberty's imperatives.

In *The Great Melody,* a magisterial study of Burke's life and ideas, Conor Cruise O'Brien adopted as his epigraph lines from Yeats's "The Seven Sages":

> American Colonies, Ireland, France, and India
> Harried, and Burke's great melody against it.[17]

---

17. Conor Cruise O'Brien, *The Great Melody: A Thematic Biography of Edmund Burke* (Chicago: University of Chicago Press, 1992), Preface.

Yeats's lines, O'Brien showed, capture the unifying spirit of Burke's political labors, which involved steady opposition to that abuse of power that consisted in the disregard by government of the fundamental requirements of liberty. As a member of Parliament Burke supported American self-government, toleration for Ireland's Catholics, and ending Warren Hastings's corrupt and cruel administration of India. These reforms may seem at odds with Burke's ferocious criticism of the French revolutionaries. But both reflect the balance of principles, interests, and goods that underwrite liberty's conservation and direct its correction.

Burke's reform efforts rested on the conviction that what a legislator particularly owed his constituents was sound judgment. In November 1774, in a speech to his supporters upon his election to Parliament from Bristol, then England's second largest city, Burke sought to dispel the popular misconception that representatives must obey their constituents' explicit instructions and mandates.[18] Representatives are obliged to vigorously advance their constituents' interests, he readily acknowledged, but they are not obliged to accept their constituents' understanding of those interests or their constituents' opinions about the policies that would best advance them. Speaking with a high sense of purpose and

---

18. Edmund Burke, "Speech to the Electors of Bristol, on His Being Declared by the Sheriffs Duly Elected One of the Representatives in Parliament for That City," *The Works of the Right Honourable Edmund Burke,* Vol. II (London: John C. Nimmo, 1887), p. 89, available at http://www.gutenberg.org/files/15198/15198-h/15198-h.htm#ELECTORS_OF_BRISTOL. See also Edmund Burke, "Speech at the Guildhall in Bristol, Previous to the Late Election" (1780), ibid., p. 382, available at http://www.gutenberg.orgfiles/15198/15198-h/15198-h.htm#GUILDHALL_IN_BRISTOL. Fourteen years later, James Madison similarly argued that the institution of representation, while rooted in the people's will, works to refine that will and bring it in line with the people's reason. See James Madison, *Federalist* Nos. 10, 49, 51, in Alexander Hamilton, James Madison, and John Jay, *The Federalist Papers,* ed. Clinton Rossiter, Introduction and Notes by Charles R. Kesler (New York: Signet Classic, 2003).

uncommon frankness to those returning him to London, Burke explained that

> it ought to be the happiness and glory of a representative to live in the strictest union, the closest correspondence, and the most unreserved communication with his constituents. Their wishes ought to have great weight with him; their opinions high respect; their business unremitted attention. It is his duty to sacrifice his repose, his *pleasures, his satisfactions, to theirs*—and above all, ever, and in all cases, to prefer their interest to his own.
>
> But, his unbiased opinion, his mature judgment, his enlightened conscience, he ought not to sacrifice to you, to any man, or to any set of men living. These he does not derive from your pleasure,—no, nor from the law and the Constitution. They are a trust from Providence, for the abuse of which he is deeply answerable. Your representative owes you, not his industry only, but his judgment, and he betrays, instead of serving you, if he sacrifices it to your opinion.[19]

The representative's responsibility to provide sound judgment stems not only from moral and religious duty but also from the division of labor in which modern representative self-government is grounded. It is the representative who is immersed in the issues of the day. It is the representative who has the opportunity to debate the fine points of legislation and to deliberate. And it is the representative who, from the perspective of the capital city, can look out beyond local purposes and prejudices to consider the long-term consequences of policy and the general good of the whole nation.

---

19. "Speech to the Electors of Bristol," p. 95.

The sound judgment that Burke champions differs greatly from the "public reason" from which today's professors of political theory and law purport to derive law and public policy. "Public reason"[20] and its operation in "deliberative democracy"[21] describe not the reason that citizens and public officials actually exercise, but rather a system of assumptions about human beings and a hierarchy of moral values that they ideally should accept. When applied to the issues of the day, the professors' theories invariably yield results that correspond to progressive policy preferences.[22] In contrast, Burke maintained that sound judgment grows out of practice; is rooted in the rich soil of moral and political life; and balances conservation and correction.

Keenly appreciative of the interests, institutions, and powers that representatives must reconcile, Burke urged his Bristol constituents to keep in mind that their bustling port city

> is but a part of a rich commercial *nation*, the interests of which
> are various, multiform, and intricate. We are members for that
> great nation, which, however, is itself but part of a great empire,
> extended by our virtue and our fortune to the farthest limits of
> the East and of the West. All these wide-spread *interests* must be
> considered,—must be compared,—must be reconciled, if pos-
> sible. We are members for a *free* country; and surely we all know
> that the machine of a free constitution is no simple thing, but as

---

20. See John Rawls, *Political Liberalism,* Expanded Edition (New York: Columbia University Press, 2005).

21. See Amy Gutmann and Dennis Thompson, *Democracy and Disagreement* (Cambridge, Mass.: Harvard University Press, 1996).

22. For an elaboration of these criticisms, see Peter Berkowitz, "The Ambiguities of Rawls's Influence," *Perspectives on Politics* Vol. 4/No. 1, March 2006, available at http://www.peterberkowitz.com/theambiguitiesofrawlsinfluence.pdf; and Berkowitz, "The Debating Society," *The New Republic,* Nov. 26, 1996, available at http://www.peterberkowitz.com/debatingsociety.htm.

intricate and as delicate as it is valuable. We are members in a great and ancient *monarchy*; and we must preserve religiously the true, legal rights of the sovereign, which form the keystone that binds together the noble and well-constructed arch of our empire and our Constitution. A constitution made up of balanced powers must ever be a critical thing.[23]

With the controversial positions he advocated for America, Ireland, and India, Burke sought to honor the representative's duty to preserve the balance under Britain's constitutional government crucial to liberty.

Burke delivered his "Speech on Conciliation with the Colonies" in the House of Commons on March 22, 1775.[24] This was ten years to the day after Parliament passed the Stamp Act, which increased taxes on the American colonists while rejecting their demands for representation, and which Burke, as a new member of Parliament, had opposed. And it was less than a month before the battles of Lexington and Concord would ignite the Revolutionary War, a dire outcome against which Burke had for many years warned. With tensions mounting in 1775, Burke insisted on the need to formulate policy with a view to actual circumstances at home and in the colonies. He urged that deliberations should proceed on the basis of an appreciation of common interests and "not according to our own imaginations, not according to abstract ideas of right, by no means according to mere general theories of government, the resort to which appears to me, in our present situ-

---

23. "Speech to the Electors of Bristol," p. 97.

24. Edmund Burke, "Speech on Conciliation with the Colonies," *The Works of the Right Honourable Edmund Burke,* Vol. II (London: John C. Nimmo, 1887), available at http://www.gutenberg.org/files/15198/15198-h/15198-h.htm# CONCILIATION_WITH_THE_COLONIES.

ation, no better than arrant trifling."[25] The most important circumstance was the deeply rooted devotion to freedom Britain shared with America.

This shared interest in freedom was tightly connected to their shared interest in prosperity. Over the previous seventy years, England's trade with the colonies had increased "no less than twelvefold," and commerce with America had come to constitute more than one-third of England's total worldwide trade.[26] America's rise and the resulting benefits to Britain were due in considerable part to London's hands-off policy: "through a wise and salutary neglect, a generous nature has been suffered to take her own way to perfection."[27] Burke argued for maintaining this hands-off policy. He viewed American exuberance, even American obstreperousness, with generosity: "I pardon something to the spirit of liberty."[28]

To preserve the colonies' vital place in the empire in the wake of the violence breaking out across the Atlantic would require "prudent management."[29] Force was to be avoided since it weakened—when it did not ruin—the object it subdued. It would be particularly counterproductive in America because liberty was the colonists' lifeblood and the decisive factor in their vital contribution to the empire. Indeed, Burke asserted, "a love of freedom is the predominating feature which marks and distinguishes"[30] the American character.

America's "fierce spirit of liberty," which only increased with the growth in the colonies' size and prosperity, arose from several

---

25. Ibid., p. 109.
26. Ibid., p. 113.
27. Ibid., p. 118.
28. Ibid.
29. Ibid.
30. Ibid., p. 120.

sources.[31] As descendants of Englishmen, Americans inherited the English notion that liberty depended on the right, exercised through representatives, to have a say in the taxes imposed upon them. The high degree of participation in the popular governments they established throughout the colonies further heightened Americans' passion for liberty. Their Protestantism, which had "sprung up in direct opposition to all the ordinary powers of the world," inclined Americans to make strong claims on behalf of "natural liberty."[32] In the South, the institution of slavery paradoxically amplified slave owners' attachment to freedom by reinforcing their identification of it with nobility and high station. Throughout the land, avid reading and study, especially of law, increased Americans' sensitivity to abuses of power and honed their arguments on liberty's behalf. And finally, the three thousand miles of ocean separating America from Parliament thwarted responsible oversight by London and weakened the colonists' willingness to submit to the central government's authority.

These powerful and diverse sources nourishing the spirit of freedom in America, according to Burke, made it all but inevitable that arguments marshaled in London against colonists' demands for greater representation—including those arguments with respectable grounds in traditional British understandings and practice—were bound to fall on deaf ears in America. Consequently, Britain had three choices: to remove the immediate cause of the dispute; to prosecute defiant Americans as criminals; or to recognize American demands for representation as unavoidable and reasonable in the circumstances and devise ways to satisfy them.

To attempt to remove the immediate cause, which was rooted in the colonists' love of liberty, would be worse than useless, con-

31. Ibid., pp. 120–127.
32. Ibid., p. 123.

tended Burke, since it would enrage the colonists and deprive
England of America's bounty.

Prosecuting the colonists for acts of resistance was no more
advisable. Taking a hard line was inconsistent with maintaining
an empire which, grounded as it was in liberty, must allow for
challenges to government policy. Crushing the colonists' resistance to authority would "teach them that the government against
which a claim of liberty is tantamount to high treason is a government to which submission is equivalent to slavery."[33]

The only reasonable option was for Britain to accommodate
American demands for greater self-government. Thus Burke
favored granting the colonists limited representation in Parliament
on questions of taxation, though not as a matter of right. With the
question of right, he wished "to have nothing at all to do."[34] The
legal question, for Burke, counted as "less than nothing."[35] Rather,
"the question with me is, not whether you have a right to render
your people miserable; but whether it is not your interest to make
them happy."[36] Statesmanship went well beyond questions of
strict legality, and it took into account much more than crude
calculations of utility. "I am not determining a point of law,"
Burke declared. "I am restoring tranquility: and the general
character and situation of a people must determine what sort of
government is fitted for them."[37] Prudent appreciation of the
spirit of liberty common to America and Britain prescribed
granting the colonists a measure of representation. And a measure of representation advanced a surpassing British interest,

---

33. Ibid., p. 137.
34. Ibid., p. 140.
35. Ibid.
36. Ibid.
37. Ibid., p. 141.

which was *"to admit the people of our colonies into an interest in the Constitution."*[38]

Such a policy involved a substantial concession. But it was a concession, asserted Burke, rooted in principles favoring the fortification of liberty and representative government that had consistently informed British government policy. Indeed, conciliation itself was "the ancient constitutional policy of this kingdom."[39] It reflected the very nature of politics:

> All government, indeed every human benefit and enjoyment, every virtue and every prudent act, is founded on compromise and barter. We balance inconveniences; we give and take; we remit some rights, that we may enjoy others; and we choose rather to be happy citizens than subtle disputants.[40]

In Burke's estimation, the balance of inconveniences involved in conciliation with America amounted to a particularly good deal for Britain. By allowing English liberties to flourish in the colonies, Britain would encourage the spirit of liberty that made both Britain and America prosperous, reinforce the spirit of liberty at home, and conserve English dominion on a long-term basis since liberty was also a dictate of justice.

Five years later, in his 1780 speech at the Bristol Guildhall, which marked the close of his career representing Bristol, Burke offered a trenchant defense of a bill intended to ease the significant disabilities England's Penal Laws imposed on Irish Catholics.[41]

---

38. Ibid.
39. Ibid., p. 154.
40. Ibid., p. 169.
41. Edmund Burke, "Speech at the Guildhall in Bristol, Previous to the Late Election," *The Works of the Right Honourable Edmund Burke,* Vol. II (London: John C. Nimmo, 1887), p. 366, available at http://www.gutenberg.org/files /15198/15198-h/15198-h.htm#GUILDHALL_IN_BRISTOL.

This was a delicate matter for Burke. His father, Richard Burke, was a Protestant who, a few years before Edmund was born in 1729, almost certainly had converted from Catholicism so he could practice law. Burke's mother, Mary Nagle, was a Catholic, as was Burke's wife of forty years, Jane. Throughout his career, Burke was highly circumspect about his Catholic connections even as his political enemies regularly attacked him as a Catholic sympathizer, a damaging charge in eighteenth-century British politics. Indeed, along with his support for free trade with Ireland and for easing penalties for debtors, Burke's advocacy of toleration of Catholics in Ireland caused the loss of his Bristol seat (he went on to represent Malton, a less powerful position). As O'Brien observed in *The Great Melody,* Burke's defense of the rights of Catholics is all the more poignant for the personal interests it implicated and all the more impressive for the political costs it exacted.

According to Burke, his critics believed that tolerance in Ireland recklessly pushed the demand for justice beyond what his constituents and Britain more generally could bear. In reply, he argued that the reforms he sought reflected the imperatives of liberty in light of the realities of British politics.

The long view, Burke maintained, was relevant to the determination of the proper public policy concerning the freedom of those who belonged to the minority faith. Appealing to his constituents' majority Protestant faith, Burke pointed out that the principle of toleration has roots in the Reformation, "one of the greatest periods of human improvement."[42] Nevertheless, pockets of intolerance in violation of Protestant principles of liberty persisted in Ireland long after the Reformation, not least in the form of the harsh restrictions imposed upon Catholics. In 1699, the Penal Laws made it a crime punishable by imprisonment to say

---

42. Ibid., p. 389.

Catholic Mass or to teach Catholicism. The Penal Laws also required Catholics to renounce their faith or forfeit their land, and set severe limits on professional advancement—limits like those faced by Burke's father.

One did not have to rely only on distinctively Protestant principles, however, to condemn the wrongs inflicted on Catholics by the Penal Laws. Universal principles, Burke asserted, also condemned them. The Penal Laws attacked human nature, crippling in their targets "the rights and feelings of humanity."[43] They had a "tendency to degrade and abase mankind, and to deprive them of that assured and liberal state of mind which alone can make us what we ought to be."[44] So terrible was the indignity that Burke would have rather

> put a man to immediate death for opinions I disliked, and so to get rid of the man and his opinions at once, than to fret him with a feverish being, tainted with the jail-distemper of a contagious servitude, to keep him above ground an animated mass of putrefaction, corrupted himself, and corrupting all about him.[45]

The repeal of the Penal Laws was necessitated both by the religious principles held by a majority of Britons and by the common humanity all men shared.

Other considerations, grounded in the events of the day, also counseled reform. With toleration gaining ground throughout Europe—in Holland, Germany, Sweden, and France—British toleration of Catholics would lend support abroad to Protestant claims to toleration in Catholic countries. And as Catholics were

---

43. Ibid., p. 391.
44. Ibid., p. 396.
45. Ibid.

Britain's best manufacturers, toleration advanced British commercial interests.

But if toleration was so important, other critics asked, why did Burke support a bill that provided only partial relief from the Penal Laws rather than their outright repeal? Because, answered Burke, prudence so counseled. While outright repeal was not politically attainable, partial relief would provide a "progressive experience."[46] By means of incremental steps, "the people would grow reconciled to toleration, when they should find, by the effects, that justice was not so irreconcilable an enemy to convenience as they had imagined."[47]

Still others objected that Parliament was acting with undue haste. Burke retorted that Parliament was proceeding too slowly,[48] taking eighty years to undertake the repair of laws that never should have been implemented. And to those who insisted monarchs posed the true threat to freedom, Burke responded that freedom was threatened from many quarters. It could be imperiled just as much by the "strongest faction,"[49] the tyranny of the majority, and indeed by the rage to rule over others that sometimes wears the mask of freedom:

> It is but too true, that the love, and even the very idea, of genuine liberty is extremely rare. It is but too true that there are many whose whole scheme of freedom is made up of pride, perverseness, and insolence. They feel themselves in a state of thraldom, they imagine that their souls are cooped and cabined

---

46. Ibid., p. 409.
47. Ibid.
48. Ibid., p. 415.
49. Ibid., p. 416.

in, unless they have some man or some body of men dependent on their mercy.[50]

Because liberty is subject to abuse in many ways and the true love of liberty is rare, the people's will must be "confined within the limits of justice,"[51] which impose toleration as a defining feature of a free society.

In his 1783 speech on Fox's East India Bill, Burke once again pressed for reforms based on the conviction that honoring the claims of liberty abroad made liberty at home more secure.[52] Attacking what he believed to be Britain's gross malfeasance in India, the speech was a high point of the cause to which he devoted the greater part of the final decade of his parliamentary career. To his many critics, it seemed that he was consumed with the issue. Indeed, Burke went to great lengths to bring to justice Warren Hastings, the first governor-general of Bengal, who effectively ruled India from 1773 to 1785. Burke led the 1787 impeachment of Hastings in the House of Commons and the eight-year prosecution of Hastings at the Bar of the House of Lords, which ended in acquittal in 1795. Even still, Burke's early entry into the controversy in his speech in support of Fox's East India Bill—Charles James Fox was leader of the Whigs but Burke conceived and drafted the bill—is a model of reasoned political analysis and advocacy. It is notable, as was his call for conciliation with America and his insistence on tolerance for Ireland's Catholics, for arguing that Britain's interest in liberty and the morality of

---

50. Ibid., pp. 416–417.
51. Ibid., p. 421.
52. Edmund Burke, "Speech on Mr. Fox's East India Bill," *The Works of the Right Honourable Edmund Burke*, Vol. II (London: John C. Nimmo, 1887), available at http://www.gutenberg.org/files/15198/15198-h/15198-h.htm# EAST_INDIA_BILL.

liberty converged, and therefore that reform was simultaneously demanded "by humanity, by justice, and by every principle of true policy."[53]

Britain's interest in robust commerce with India, Burke argued, was inseparable from "the interest and well-being of the people of India."[54] But the British East India Company—established in 1600 by Queen Elizabeth I to promote trade—had gravely abused its power and ruthlessly exploited its prerogatives. It trampled on native-born Indians' rights and enervated the country. And in the process, the East India Company eroded British morals and undermined Britain's national interest. Consequently, Burke believed that restoring Indians' liberty was a requirement of British self-government: "every means effectual to preserve India from oppression is a guard to preserve the British Constitution from its worst corruption."[55]

The bill Burke championed aimed to alter the charter that established the East India Company's status as a private company governing India. It would give Parliament responsibility for overseeing the company. Burke's refutation of the charge that the reform represented an "attack on the chartered rights of men"[56] is of special interest because of its account of the political significance of natural rights and because of the analysis it leads to on the circumstances that justify fundamental alteration of an established institution of government.

Burke contended that by invoking the East India Company's chartered rights to prevent government intervention, opponents of reform confused the rights created by government with the universal rights governments are established to secure:

---

53. Ibid., p. 433.
54. Ibid., p. 434.
55. Ibid., p. 436.
56. Ibid., p. 437.

The rights of *men*—that is to say, the natural rights of mankind— are indeed sacred things; and if any public measure is proved mischievously to affect them, the objection ought to be fatal to that measure, even if no charter at all could be set up against it. If these natural rights are further affirmed and declared by express covenants, if they are clearly defined and secured against chicane, against power and authority, by written instruments and positive engagements, they are in a still better condition: they partake not only of the sanctity of the object so secured, but of that solemn public faith itself which secures an object of such importance. Indeed, this formal recognition, by the sovereign power, of an original right in the subject, can never be subverted, but by rooting up the holding radical principles of government, and even of society itself.[57]

Very much in keeping with the larger liberal tradition, Burke held that to be most politically effective, natural rights, which preexist and set standards for political life, require translation through legal codes into concrete guarantees.

What are properly called *"the chartered rights of men"* are those natural rights that are explicitly affirmed in fundamental legal documents. The Magna Carta, "a charter to restrain power and to destroy monopoly," was for Burke an outstanding example. In contrast, "The East India charter is a charter to establish monopoly and to create power."[58] It worked to "suspend the natural rights of mankind at large,"[59] allowing the company to administer, as if it were a state power, an enormous territory vital to the commercial interests of Britain as well as to manage

---

57. Ibid.
58. Ibid., p. 438.
59. Ibid.

"the lives and fortunes of thirty millions of their fellow-creatures."[60] However, the political power to rule over another is not a natural right. To the contrary, it is "wholly artificial, and for so much a derogation from the natural equality of mankind at large, ought to be some way or other exercised ultimately for their benefit."[61]

The East India Company had enjoyed a trust. By betraying the lawful purposes that brought it into being, the company had nullified the trust. In view of the company's "plenitude of despotism, tyranny, and corruption," Parliament, Burke argued, was obliged to reassert its responsibility for the equitable and efficient administration of India, to provide "a real chartered security for *the rights of men*" that the company had "cruelly violated."[62]

Burke recognized that the revision of the East India Company's charter he sought was drastic. He justified the drastic reform on the grounds that the East India Company had long persisted in drastic abuses. But the reform, he emphasized, was in no way based on an *a priori* argument against endowing a private company with the political power to administer a vast nation:

> With my particular ideas and sentiments, I cannot go that way to work. I feel an insuperable reluctance in giving my hand to destroy any established institution of government, upon a theory, however plausible it may be.[63]

Furthermore, no established institution of government, Burke maintained, should be repudiated for the mere existence of abuses

---

60. Ibid., p. 439.
61. Ibid.
62. Ibid., p. 441.
63. Ibid., p. 442.

in the exercise of its powers, because "there are, and must be, abuses in all governments."[64]

Because of the wisdom embodied in established institutions, Burke held that sweeping change should be contemplated only as a last resort to protect the most basic individual rights and vital national interests.[65] Accordingly, fundamental alteration of established institutions of government would have to meet exacting criteria:

> 1st, The object affected by the abuse should be great and important. 2nd, The abuse affecting this great object ought to be a great abuse. 3d, It ought to be habitual, and not accidental. 4th, It ought to be utterly incurable in the body as it now stands constituted.[66]

And the evidence concerning the object, greatness, regularity, and implacableness of the abuse must be as clear as "the light of the sun."[67] The bulk of Burke's speech on Fox's East India Bill delves into the nitty-gritty of the British administration of India, supplying ample evidence demonstrating that the conduct of the East India Company under the direction of Governor-General Hastings represented an extreme abuse of power that obliged Parliament to implement far-reaching reforms.

---

64. Ibid., p. 443.

65. Or, as he argues in distinguishing the Revolution of 1688 from the French Revolution, sweeping change should be in response only to "a grave and overruling necessity" and should be undertaken "with infinite reluctance, as under that most rigorous of all laws." *Reflections on the Revolution in France,* p. 267; see also pp. 311–312.

66. "Speech on Mr. Fox's East India Bill," p. 442.

67. Ibid.

Burke's arguments in behalf of reform of British policy toward India are of a piece with those he put forward in behalf of reform of British policy toward America and Ireland. They reflect the exacting standard of statesmanship devoted to liberty he espoused in the *Reflections*:

> A disposition to preserve, and an ability to improve, taken together, would be my standard of a statesman. Everything else is vulgar in the conception, perilous in the execution.[68]

And by this exacting standard, Burke's arguments in the name of liberty in favor of reform are of a piece with his arguments in the name of liberty against the revolution in France.

Liberty and Political Moderation

The need in free societies to combine and reconcile the principles of conservation and correction imposes formidable demands on the people and on office holders. To be sure, under government of all sorts, policy and law must constantly be adjusted, balanced, and calibrated in light of changing circumstances. But liberty guarantees that circumstances will always be changing, and in fact liberty tends to accelerate the pace of change. One manifestation of the larger challenge is the famous tension between conservatism and capitalism: Capitalism's constant quest for newer and better products and techniques of production to achieve ever greater profits, combined with the affluence and luxury that free markets bring, demote tradition, disrupt order, and weaken the virtues of mind and character—such as self-restraint, industriousness, and thrift—that support free markets and free political institutions.

---

68. *Reflections on the Revolution in France*, p. 440; see also pp. 455–460.

The larger challenge is rooted in the passions and bound up with a paradox of freedom. Liberty excites the human love of novelty—for how can I be free if I must submit to the same old routines? And it goads the human love of dominion—for how can I be free if others defy my will? By simultaneously encouraging an aversion to authority and a desire for mastery, freedom also tends to provoke a backlash against freedom. The result in free societies is the generation of extreme and conflicting types: radicals who seek to extend government's rule over others in the name of equality while freeing themselves from rules, and reactionaries who strive to reinstate traditional forms of authority, not only on themselves but on the rest of society. Liberty unrestrained fosters varieties of immoderation. Consequently, a government devoted to conserving and correcting freedom will require particular prudence in the art of balancing, or political moderation.[69]

The virtue of political moderation is often mistaken for a compromise with virtue, a softening of belief, a diluting of passion, a weakening of will, even an outright vice. But those are examples not of political moderation but of the failure to achieve it. Moderation in politics is not a retreat from the fullness of life but an embrace of it. Political moderation is called into action by the awareness of the variety of enduring moral and political principles; the substantial limits on what we can know and how effectively and justly we can act; the range of legitimate individual interests; the multiplicity of valuable human undertakings and ends; and the quest to discern a common good in light of which we can make moral distinctions and establish political priorities.[70] Political mod-

---

69. For further reflections on the paradox of freedom, see Peter Berkowitz, "The Liberal Spirit in America," *Policy Review*, Aug./Sept. 2003, available at http://www.hoover.org/publications/policy-review/article/7229.

70. See Harry M. Clor, *On Moderation: Defending an Ancient Virtue in a Modern World* (Waco, Texas: Baylor University Press, 2008), chap. 1.

eration underlies self-government understood as a free people's rule over itself and as the individual's mastery of his conduct.

Nevertheless, the virtue of political moderation will always serve as an inviting target for demagogues who seek to exploit the passion for purity in politics. In the *Reflections,* Burke warned that one who supports "a scheme of liberty soberly limited" is likely to be accused of lacking "fidelity to his cause."[71] The purists' attack on the appeal to reason and the exercise of restraint in behalf of freedom will not end there:

> Moderation will be stigmatized as the virtue of cowards, and compromise as the prudence of traitors,—until, in hopes of preserving the credit which may enable him to temper and moderate on some occasions, the popular leader is obliged to become active in propagating doctrines and establishing powers that will afterwards defeat any sober purpose at which he ultimately might have aimed.[72]

Because of the perennial need to stand firmly against the common slander that political moderation is a feeble disguise for weak-kneed betrayal of principle, political moderation is inseparable from political courage.

Burke's devotion to political moderation was hardly evident to all observers in his time and would have been disputed by many. Consequently, he was compelled to clarify his beliefs about it. In the final paragraph of the *Reflections,* written twenty-five years after he was first elected to Parliament and four years before his retirement, Burke declared that he had been one "almost the whole of whose public exertion has been a struggle for the

---

71. *Reflections on the Revolution in France,* p. 560.
72. Ibid.

liberty of others."[73] Aware that his attack on the French Revolution gave rise to the appearance of inconsistency, he made sense of the seeming contradictions by explaining the underlying reality. Invoking a classical image, he characterized his words and actions as those of a statesman

> who would preserve consistency by varying his means to secure the unity of his end,—and, when the equipoise of the vessel in which he sails may be endangered by overloading it upon one side, is desirous of carrying the small weight of his reasons to that which may preserve its equipoise.[74]

To conserve liberty at a time when the French revolutionaries made extravagant claims in its behalf, Burke fervently championed the claims of tradition, order, and virtue. And when his countrymen failed to grasp its imperatives in their affairs abroad in America, Ireland, and India, he passionately urged reforms that enlarged liberty's sphere.

The conservative side of the larger liberal tradition displays variations on the political moderation contained in Burke's insistence on the importance of combining and reconciling the principles of conservation and correction. In *The Wealth of Nations* in 1776, Burke's contemporary Adam Smith examined the mutual dependence of economic life and virtue. Smith saw that the market economy, which brought prosperity and nourished political liberty, both rewarded moral virtues—rationality, industry, ingenuity,

73. Ibid., p. 563.

74. Ibid. For Burke's insistence on his consistency, see also "An Appeal from the New to the Old Whigs," *The Works of the Right Honourable Edmund Burke,* Vol. IV (London: John C. Nimmo, 1887), pp. 92–103, available at http://www .gutenberg.org/files/15700/15700-h/15700-h.htm#APPEAL; and "Letter to a Noble Lord," ibid., pp. 185–189.

and self-discipline—and corrupted workers' character by condemning them to monotonous labor. He therefore contended that
government must take action by, for example, providing education for workers and limiting the workplace demands imposed on
them by manufacturers. In *Democracy in America,* the first volume
of which appeared in 1835 and the second in 1840, Alexis de
Tocqueville argued that in the modern era democracy had become
necessary and just and that while it fostered a certain simplicity
and straightforwardness in manners, it also encouraged selfishness,
envy, immediate gratification, and lazy acceptance of state authority. To secure liberty, which he believed essential for a well-lived
life, it would be necessary to preserve within democracy those
nongovernmental institutions—family, religious faith, and civic
associations of many sorts—that counteracted democracy's delete-
rious tendencies. Family, faith, and civic associations taught moral
virtue, connected individuals to higher purposes, and broadened
their appreciation of their self-interest to include their debts to
forebears, bonds to fellow citizens, and obligations to future generations. John Stuart Mill, an admirer of Tocqueville whose
voluminous writings feature conspicuously conservative and progressive dimensions, made the case in 1859 in *On Liberty* that
liberty served "the permanent interests of man as a progressive
being."[75] At the same time, he distinguished between the use and
abuse of freedom; defended a rigorous education continuing
through university and combining science and humanities to equip
individuals for freedom's opportunities and demands; and favored
political institutions that, while grounded in the consent of the
governed, were designed to improve the likelihood that elections

---

75. John Stuart Mill, *J.S. Mill: On Liberty and Other Writings,* ed. Stefan
Collini (Cambridge: Cambridge University Press, 1989), p. 14.

would bring individuals of outstanding moral and intellectual virtue to public office.

If a liberal in the large sense is one who believes that the aim of politics is to secure liberty, then Smith, Tocqueville, and Mill are, like Burke, exemplary members of the liberal tradition. Because of their common appreciation that free societies expose individuals to influences that corrode moral and political order and enervate the virtues on which liberty depends, their ideas fortify the conservative side of the liberal tradition. Because of their shared understanding that limits must be imposed on government to protect individual liberty but that those limits must not sap the energy or impair the authority government needs to secure liberty, their account of self-government emphasizes striking a balance between competing and essential principles. Their political moderation is a reflection of their passion for freedom and their reasoned understanding of the complex conditions that sustain it. *The Federalist,* the masterpiece of American political thought, embraces the conservative brand of liberal self-government they epitomize and constitutionalizes it.

CHAPTER **3**

The Federalist:
Constitutionalizing Liberty

S carcely a detail of constitutional design escaped lively and learned debate at the Constitutional Convention in the spring and sweltering summer of 1787. Yet all the delegates in Philadelphia readily agreed on the Constitution's leading principles: government's power derived from the consent of the governed; its preeminent aim was to secure individual liberty or the rights shared equally by all; and limits must be built into government to honor consent and secure liberty.

Indeed, the consensus about government's leading principles was so wide and deep in America during the founding era that in the great ratifying debates that took place during the fall of 1787 and well into 1788, the consensus encompassed the Constitution's worthy opponents, who came to be known as the Anti-Federalists. Their major objection was that the proposed limits for the new national government were too few and too ineffective to meet the requirements of republicanism, which was generally understood as government whose authority was rooted in the people and whose purpose was to advance the people's good by safeguarding their liberty. The size, structure, powers, and distance from the people of the national government outlined in the Constitution, the Anti-Federalists contended, posed an intolerable threat to the people's freedom. The Constitution would inevitably overwhelm the states, invade people's rights, and undermine the virtues that republican government demanded.[1]

For their part, the Constitution's proponents agreed in principle with the Anti-Federalists about the threats a strong national government posed to liberty and self-government. Despite the dangers, the founders maintained that the Articles of Confederation, the charter of government under which Americans had been living, had to be replaced because they suffered from irreparable weaknesses. Agreed to by the Continental Congress in 1777 in the midst of the Revolutionary War and ratified in 1781, two years before the Treaty of Paris brought the war to an end, the Articles of Confederation left the Continental Congress unable to effectively provide for the common defense, conduct diplomacy, collect taxes, regulate commerce, and adjudicate disputes that crossed state boundaries. A substantially strengthened national government, the champions of the Constitution argued, was necessary to perform the tasks crucial to preserving the union. And, they believed, preservation of the union was vital because it provided the best means of preserving the people's liberty.

Sharing the Anti-Federalists' fears about government power, the framers devised diverse restraints to control the larger and stronger national government they presented to the American people for ratification in the form of the Constitution. A principal instrument of restraint was federalism, or the establishment, in the interest of individual liberty, of a judicious balance in the division of labor between the national government and state governments.

In a letter to George Washington a month before delegates gathered in Philadelphia, James Madison placed the challenge of

---

1. See *The Anti-Federalist Papers and the Constitutional Convention Debates,* ed. Ralph Ketcham (New York: Signet Classics, 2003).

federalism front and center. On April 16, 1787, Madison—who because of his central role at Philadelphia earned the title "father of the Constitution"—wrote:

> Conceiving that an individual independence of the States is utterly irreconcileable with their aggregate sovereignty; and that a consolidation of the whole into one simple republic would be as inexpedient as it is unattainable, I have sought for some middle ground, which may at once support a due supremacy of the national authority, and not exclude the local authorities wherever they can be subordinately useful.[2]

Madison offered several proposals for attaining some middle ground between individual independence of the states and one simple republic composed of the people of all the states. The proposals aimed at strengthening the national government by giving it a variety of new powers: to operate without the regular intervention of state governments; to exercise ultimate authority in matters requiring uniformity, including regulation of trade and naturalization; to veto state legislation; and to wield supremacy in judicial matters. Not all of Madison's proposals were adopted: the Constitution does not grant the national government a veto over state legislation, though state legislation must be consistent with the Constitution and federal law. But Madison's determination to balance the claims of "local authorities" with "a due supremacy of the national authority" was embraced as a guiding principle at Philadelphia and woven into the fabric of the Constitution.

A well-balanced federalism, however, would not be sufficient to attain a middle ground between the extremes of unqualified state

---

2. Letter from James Madison to George Washington, available at http://press-pubs.uchicago.edu/founders/documents/v1ch8s6.html.

sovereignty and a single pure republic. "A Government composed of such extensive powers" as Madison envisaged would also itself need to be "well organized and balanced."[3] The essential balance would have to be achieved not only between the national government and state governments but within the national government itself (and within state governments).

The balance Madison sought amounted to more than providing competing interests the room to maneuver. It went beyond allowing policy preferences from different political perspectives to be considered and contested. It strove to give rival and worthy political principles—such as individual rights and majority will, energy and stability, limited and enumerated powers and flexibility in governance—their due weight. The framers' aim was to constitutionalize liberty by institutionalizing political moderation.

Contemporary Perspectives, Classical Roots, Founding Compromises

The balancing of diverse principles, or political moderation, that the Constitution incorporates into the fundamental structure of government is often misunderstood, if not overlooked, because of immoderate views that are brought to bear on it. Many of today's progressives subscribe to dubious opinions inherited from the original progressivism that arose at the end of the nineteenth century and flourished in the first two decades of the twentieth century. They tend to understand the Constitution primarily in terms of checks and balances, which they conceive of in a crude Newtonian or mechanical sense. Moreover, they are likely to suppose that advances in morality and science have greatly reduced the need to limit government power, which the framers considered of para-

---

3. Ibid.

mount importance. And progressives are inclined to blame the Constitution's cumbersome lawmaking apparatus for blocking what they regard as urgent projects of social and political transformation.[4]

These progressive criticisms frequently rest on mistaken notions of the purpose, structure, and operation of the Constitution, and typically misidentify the true sources of progressive frustration.

First, the Constitution's scheme of checks and balances also facilitates cooperation by blending powers so that in limited but consequential ways, each branch of government is involved in the operation of the other two. Second, the evidence is overwhelmingly against those who believe that human nature has undergone any fundamental alteration since the eighteenth century or, more to the point, that self-interest, pride, ambition, greed, envy, fear, and the whole panoply of destabilizing passions the framers fortified the Constitution to withstand have ceased to interfere with the exercise of reason by citizens and their representatives. And third, progressives seldom contemplate that their inability to assemble enduring electoral majorities in behalf of progressive political goals reflects both lack of solid majority support and constitutional constraints designed to encourage deliberation in the legislative process.

In contrast to progressives who typically seek to overcome the Constitution, conservatives characteristically strive to recover and renew it. Conservative scholars of political theory have been at the forefront of the quest over the last half-century to acquire an

---

4. For outspoken statements of the Constitution's supposed grave defects, see Sanford Levinson, *Our Undemocratic Constitution: Where the Constitution Goes Wrong and How We the People Can Correct It* (New York: Oxford University Press, 2008), and Levinson, "Our Imbecilic Constitution," *The New York Times,* May 28, 2012, available at http://campaignstops.blogs.nytimes.com /2012/05/28/our-imbecilic-constitution.

accurate understanding of the letter and spirit of the Constitution, including an appreciation of the Anti-Federalist thinkers who opposed it in the name of liberty. Conservative legal scholars have championed the doctrine of originalism, which grounds the authority of federal judges to strike down legislation as unconstitutional in a historically informed understanding of the Constitution's original meaning. And members of the Tea Party movement, who rallied around conservative candidates in the November 2010 midterm elections, have popularized the return to the Constitution, enthusiastically calling for a renewal of a constitutional conservatism that has at its core a dedication to the central constitutional principle of limited government.

Conservatives, however, are not immune to immoderate views about the Constitution. Whereas progressives are inclined to disparage it, conservatives tend to idealize it. The conservative temptation has been to ascribe to the Constitution a purity it never possessed and never could have attained. In succumbing, conservatives neglect the spirit of political moderation that gives strength and resilience to the political institutions the Constitution establishes.

The spirit of political moderation that animates the Constitution must not be confused with the progressive celebration of the "living Constitution." Progressives usually invoke the idea of the living Constitution as an invitation to judges to find in the Constitution's vaguer formulations—"due process of law," "equal protection," the prohibition on "cruel and unusual punishment," and the power to "regulate commerce...among the several states"— malleable moral and political values. These values, they contend, authorize courts to strike down laws they think unwise, unjust, or at odds with the fundamental requirements of democracy, though not apparently in conflict with the Constitution's text, structure, and the history of its framing and ratification; or authorize courts to uphold laws that, while in conflict with the

Constitution's text, structure, and the history of its framing and ratification, are in progressives' opinion wise, just, or required by democratic theory.[5] In contrast, the political moderation that animates the Constitution is found in its text and structure and the history of its framing and ratification. Supreme Court Justice Antonin Scalia has remarked that he prefers a dead Constitution[6]— a salutary preference in the face of progressives' inclination, in the guise of respecting the Constitution, to infuse it with partisan moral values and policy preferences. But in reality the American Constitution promotes the spirit of balance. The balance it strikes among competing political principles and the imperative to balance that its design proclaims are of course highly relevant to the judicial task. The relevance, however, extends well beyond the judiciary; it applies also to the activities of the legislative and executive branches, to citizens' exercise of their rights and discharge of their responsibilities, and indeed to every aspect of self-government in a free society.

The framers of the Constitution incorporated political moderation into the institutions of government in novel and potent ways. But they were by no means the first to recognize the importance of political moderation to good government. Indeed, the Constitution also partakes of the old practice of weaving together

---

5. For an impressive progressive effort to square the circle by showing that the Constitution embodies progressive values and, where it does not require, is quite compatible with the contemporary progressive agenda, see Jack M. Balkin, *Living Originalism* (Cambridge, Mass.: Harvard University Press, 2011). For a critique, see Peter Berkowitz, "Reading into the Constitution," *Policy Review,* June/July 2012, available at http://www.hoover.org/publications/policy-review /article/118436.

6. Interview with Justice Scalia, "Scalia Vigorously Defends a 'Dead' Constitution," *All Things Considered,* April 28, 2008, available at http://www.npr .org/templates/story/story.php?storyId=90011526.

diverse human elements and political principles, which Plato and Aristotle taught was the quintessential political art.[7]

In accordance with the classical understanding, the framers recognized that to perform their tasks well, legislatures, the executive, and judges would require different skills and qualities, because the political institutions created by the Constitution incorporate a variety of political principles. The House of Representatives is closest to the people and is the most democratic and boisterous; representatives are apportioned on the basis of population and every two years they stand for election in relatively small districts. The Senate, in which states are represented equally and whose members serve six-year terms, is more aristocratic and staid; it is designed for thorough deliberation and involves weightier responsibilities, providing advice and consent on treaties and executive branch appointments and trying all officials whom the House votes to impeach. The president's energy and unity reflect king-like qualities that come into play in the enforcement of the law, the conduct of foreign affairs, and the exercise of commander-in-chief powers. Independent judges, who are appointed for life, represent the operation within the federal government of judgment about law that is relatively insulated from politics.

The imperative to balance extends to the compromises that the founders adopted because they needed to obtain the requisite signatures at the Constitutional Convention and ultimately win ratification of the new charter of government. The most important structurally, and the most in keeping with the underlying spirit of the Constitution, was the so-called Great Compromise. Borrowing elements from the Virginia Plan and the New Jersey Plan, it

---

7. For the need to mix and combine in proper proportions, see Plato, *Republic,* Book VI 500b–501c; and Aristotle, *Politics,* Book V 1309a30–1310a35, and Book VI 1319b35–1321a1.

was responsible for establishing the legislative branch as bi-cameral, with states receiving proportional representation in the House and equal representation in the Senate.[8] The most notorious of these compromises, and the most antithetical to the Constitution's underlying spirit, was the fateful compromise on slavery.[9]

Although it never uses the terms "slave" or "slavery," the Constitution gave the pernicious practice legal sanction. Article I, Section 2, counts those who were neither "free Persons" nor "Indians not taxed" as three-fifths of a person in determining representation and direct taxes.[10] Article I, Section 9, prohibits Congress from interfering with the "importation" of "persons" before 1808. And Article IV, Section 2, provides for the return of "a Person held to Service or Labour in one State" who had escaped into another state. Yet, as Abraham Lincoln argued, by refusing to use the terms "slave" and "slavery," the Constitution implicitly declares that their legal recognition was an ugly necessity.[11] Moreover, by insti-

---

8. For an incisive account, see Jack N. Rakove, *Original Meanings: Politics and Ideas in the Making of the Constitution* (New York: Vintage, 1997), pp. 57–93.

9. For a penetrating analysis, see Harry V. Jaffa, *Crisis of the House Divided: An Interpretation of the Lincoln-Douglas Debates,* 50th Anniversary Edition (Chicago: University of Chicago Press, 2007).

10. This provision is often misunderstood. The southern states wanted slaves to count as full persons, thus increasing the southern states' representation in the House of Representatives and the Electoral College. The northern states did not want the slaves to be counted at all, not because they denied the slaves' humanity, but because they believed that slaveholding states should not be rewarded with increased power in the federal government.

11. "I particularly object to the NEW position which the avowed principle of this Nebraska law gives to slavery in the body politic. I object to it because it assumes that there CAN be MORAL RIGHT in the enslaving of one man by another. I object to it as a dangerous dalliance for a free people—a sad evidence that, feeling prosperity we forget right—that liberty, as a principle, we have ceased to revere. I object to it because the fathers of the republic eschewed, and rejected it. The argument of 'Necessity' was the only argument they ever admitted in favor of slavery; and so far, and so far only as it carried them, did they ever

tutionalizing as a governing moral and political principle the self-evident truth of the Declaration of Independence that all human beings are by nature free and equal, the Constitution condemns slavery as a violation of fundamental rights and laid the ground-work for its eventual elimination after the Civil War by means of the Thirteenth, Fourteenth, and Fifteenth Amendments.[12]

---

go. They found the institution among us, which they could not help; and they cast blame upon the British King for having permitted its introduction. BEFORE the constitution, they prohibited its introduction into the north-western Territory—the only country we owned, then free from it. AT the framing and adoption of the constitution, they forebore to so much as mention the word 'slave' or 'slavery' in the whole instrument." Abraham Lincoln, "Speech on the Kansas-Nebraska Act," October 16, 1854, in *Abraham Lincoln, Speeches and Writings 1832–1858* (New York: The Library of America, 1989), p. 337.

12. "Chief Justice Taney, in his opinion in the Dred Scott case, admits that the language of the Declaration is broad enough to include the whole human family, but he and Judge Douglas argue that the authors of that instrument did not intend to include negroes, by the fact that they did not at once, actually place them on an equality with the whites. Now this grave argument comes to just nothing at all, by the other fact, that they did not at once, *or ever afterwards*, actually place all white people on an equality with one or another. And this is the staple argument of both the Chief Justice and the Senator, for doing this obvious violence to the plain unmistakable language of the Declaration. I think the authors of that notable instrument intended to include *all* men, but they did not intend to declare all men equal *in all* respects. They did not mean to say all were equal in color, size, intellect, moral developments, or social capacity. They defined with tolerable distinctness, in what respects they did consider all men created equal—equal in 'certain inalienable rights, among which are life, liberty, and the pursuit of happiness.' This they said, and this meant. They did not mean to assert the obvious untruth, that all were then actually enjoying that equality, nor yet, that they were about to confer it immediately upon them. In fact they had no power to confer such a boon. They meant simply to declare the *right*, so that the *enforcement* of it might follow as fast as circumstances should permit. They meant to set up a standard maxim for free society, which should be familiar to all, and revered by all; constantly looked to, constantly labored for, and even though never perfectly attained, constantly approximated, and thereby con-stantly spreading and deepening its influence, and augmenting the happiness and value of life to all people of all colors everywhere. The assertion that 'all men are created equal' was of no practical use in effecting our separation from Great

The Constitution's compromise with slavery does not belong to the highest form of political moderation because it did not involve the balance of worthy principles. Nor does it reflect the balancing of reputable public policies or the clash of legitimate interests. Rather, it involves the balancing of a worthy goal, the preservation of a union devoted to liberty, with an ugly necessity, acquiescence to southern states' nonnegotiable demand for the preservation of a hateful institution. In the end, only a bloody civil war could pry the South loose from it. Still, by compromising with an ugly necessity on terms that favored freedom, the Constitution, even at its low point, vindicated the claims of political moderation.[13]

Britain; and it was placed in the Declaration, not for that, but for future use. Its authors meant it to be, thank God, it is now proving itself, a stumbling block to those who in after times might seek to turn a free people back into the hateful paths of despotism. They knew the proneness of prosperity to breed tyrants, and they meant when such should re-appear in this fair land and commence their vocation they should find left for them at least one hard nut to crack." Abraham Lincoln, "Speech on Dred Scott Decision," June 26, 1857, ibid., pp. 398–399.

13. So James Madison argues in *Federalist* No. 42: "It were doubtless to be wished, that the power of prohibiting the importation of slaves had not been postponed until the year 1808, or rather that it had been suffered to have immediate operation. But it is not difficult to account, either for this restriction on the general government, or for the manner in which the whole clause is expressed. It ought to be considered as a great point gained in favor of humanity, that a period of twenty years may terminate forever, within these States, a traffic which has so long and so loudly upbraided the barbarism of modern policy; that within that period, it will receive a considerable discouragement from the federal government, and may be totally abolished, by a concurrence of the few States which continue the unnatural traffic, in the prohibitory example which has been given by so great a majority of the Union. Happy would it be for the unfortunate Africans, if an equal prospect lay before them of being redeemed from the oppressions of their European brethren! Attempts have been made to pervert this clause into an objection against the Constitution, by representing it on one side as a criminal toleration of an illicit practice, and on another as calculated to prevent voluntary and beneficial emigrations from Europe to America. I mention these misconstructions, not with a view to give them an answer, for they deserve none, but as specimens of the manner and spirit in which some have

The Federalist *and the Ambiguities of Self-Government*

The case for balance on behalf of liberty and for ratifying the Constitution as an exemplary embodiment of that balance was developed most forcefully and authoritatively in *The Federalist,* a collection of eighty-five essays that originally appeared in New York newspapers between October 1787 and August 1788. The essays were the brainchild of Alexander Hamilton, who had been one of New York's delegates to the Constitutional Convention and would become the first United States Secretary of the Treasury; he contributed nearly two-thirds of the total. He enlisted two other statesmen in the ambitious undertaking. John Jay, then Secretary of Foreign Affairs under the Continental Congress and later the first Chief Justice of the Supreme Court, contributed a handful of papers. And James Madison, who represented Virginia at the Constitutional Convention and would go on to serve as the fourth president of the United States, contributed almost one-third, including several of the most significant. All the essays were published under the pseudonym Publius, to indicate their unity of purpose and the civic inspiration the American founders drew from a founder of the Roman Republic.

While *The Federalist* has deservedly become a classic work of political philosophy, it is by no means a comprehensive treatise on politics. It does not, for example, systematically discuss religion, tradition, virtue, the family, community, education, economics,

---

thought fit to conduct their opposition to the proposed government." See *The Federalist,* No. 42, in Alexander Hamilton, James Madison, and John Jay, *The Federalist Papers,* ed. Clinton Rossiter, Introduction and Notes by Charles R. Kesler (New York: Signet Classics, 2003), pp. 262–263. All subsequent citations to individual papers will be to this print edition. *The Federalist Papers* are also available online individually at http://avalon.law.yale.edu/subject_menus/fed.asp.

or the cultural presuppositions of self-government. Nor is that a surprise. The authors' practical task was paramount: they undertook to explain the operations of the Constitution and how it translated political principles into sturdy and flexible political institutions, and thereby to persuade citizens of the state of New York that supporting the Constitution was vital to their interests and indispensable to their rights. Of course, as a political tract for the time, *The Federalist* did not refrain here and there from polemical overstatement and understatement. But it would be a great error to think of *The Federalist* as merely a polemical political tract. The authors chose to make their case for ratification by showing how the Constitution, in many cases in and through its compromises, weighed universal features of human nature and fashioned political institutions that conformed to the enduring requirements of self-government.

The Constitution's institutionalization of political moderation depended on innovations. These, Hamilton boldly proclaimed in *Federalist* No. 9, are rooted in principles that should be of interest to all "enlightened friends of liberty."[14] Thanks to "great improvement" in the modern era of "the science of politics," more effective responses had been developed to the age-old challenge of republican government.[15] The perennial problem was how to preserve the virtues of republics—liberty and self-government—while controlling the vice of instability that plagued regimes devoted to freedom and equality and eventually destroyed them. Improvements were at hand, according to Hamilton, because of progress in understanding "the efficacy of various principles" that "were either not known at all, or imperfectly known to the ancients."[16]

---

14. *The Federalist*, No. 9, p. 67.
15. Ibid.
16. Ibid.

Thanks to this progress, the Constitution would achieve a balance unprecedented in the annals of self-government, keeping government that was grounded in the consent of the governed within its proper limits, while furnishing it with the energy—or capacity to act swiftly and decisively—and the authority to effectively perform the functions indispensable to securing liberty. Prominent among the innovations were the separation of powers, checks and balances, an independent judiciary, elected legislative representatives, and an enlargement in the polity's geographical extent and population. These were all "wholly new discoveries, or have made their principal progress towards perfection in modern times."[17] They would provide "means, and powerful means, by which the excellences of republican government may be retained and its imperfections lessened or avoided."[18]

The result, Hamilton argued in an echo of Madison's April 1787 letter to Washington, was "a confederate republic" that combined the benefits of local and national sovereignty.[19] More precisely, as Madison observed in *Federalist* No. 39, the Constitution creates a government that is both federal, in that it unites sovereign states, and national, in that certain of its limited and enumerated powers reach the people in their individual capacities directly and not based on their state citizenship.[20] In another echo of Madison's letter—and in anticipation of points Madison would make in subsequent installments of *The Federalist* about the "mixed constitution"[21] and "compound republic"[22] created by the Constitution—Hamilton observed that within that mix, the Constitution

---

17. Ibid.
18. Ibid.
19. Ibid., p. 69.
20. *The Federalist*, No. 39, pp. 236–243.
21. *The Federalist*, No. 40, p. 243.
22. *The Federalist*, No. 51, p. 320.

erects a national government that itself contains a balance of competing principles. By joining energy and efficiency to accountability to the people and respect for their rights, the Constitution combines "the advantages of monarchy with those of republicanism"[23] without departing from republican political principles.[24]

The need for the political moderation that suffuses the Constitution's institutional design arises from the ambiguities of self-government. According to *The Federalist*, these reflect the ambiguities of human nature. Human beings are by nature free and equal, but equality in natural rights is accompanied by inequality in natural gifts and abilities. Human beings are also endowed with passion and reason, but since the passion for reason tends to be weak, passion often gets the better of reason. Men and women are capable of disciplining passions by means of education—in the narrow sense of literacy and general knowledge and in the broader sense of formation of character. They can also enlarge their understanding of private interest by appreciating its convergence over the long run with the public good. Through the exercise of the virtues—starting with self-control, rationality, and industry—they are able to bring their conduct in line with an enlightened understanding of their true interests. The Constitution seeks to economize on virtue because while necessary to self-government, virtue is a scarce resource that government has little competence to cultivate or authority to regulate.

Since choice is essential to admirable deeds, dignity, and happiness, virtue presupposes liberty. Conversely, liberty presupposes

---

23. *The Federalist*, No. 9, p. 69.
24. On the differences between the president and a king, see *The Federalist*, No. 69, pp. 414–421. For a shrewd study of how the Constitution obtained on republican terms the energy associated with monarchy, see Harvey C. Mansfield Jr., *Taming the Prince: The Ambivalence of Modern Executive Power* (New York: Free Press, 1989), pp. 121–298.

virtue, because maintaining the institutions of a free society—political, economic, and cultural—is hard work that requires citizens to exercise excellences of mind and character. Since religion was considered an indispensable teacher of virtue, liberty for the founders also presupposed faith,[25] which in eighteenth-century America mainly meant Protestant Christianity. However, neither virtue nor salvation was properly the aim of politics because permitting government to take responsibility for them would invite infringement of rights and government intrusion into the private sphere where it lacked knowledge, means, and legitimacy.

Contrary to the canard popularized by its academic critics and by some of its scholarly supporters, the Constitution and the larger liberal tradition do not limit government's responsibility for virtue because of theoretical opinions about the opposition between freedom and virtue, skeptical doubts concerning virtue's reality, or relativist certainties about its nonexistence. Rather, the Constitution restricts government's role in shaping opinion, instilling habits of heart and mind, and forming character in order to safeguard individual freedom. This freedom, it was widely understood at the time of the founding, enabled individuals to discharge their responsibility to maintain themselves and to care for their families and their religious communities, where virtue was principally cultivated.[26]

The framers knew that even in the best of circumstances virtue would be in short supply, and that a constitution devoted to protecting liberty and derived from the will of the people would give vice abundant opportunity to flourish. To endure, such a constitution would have to provide through its "extent and structure," in

---

25. For a classic statement, see George Washington's "Farewell Address" (1796), available at http://avalon.law.yale.edu/18th_century/washing.asp.

26. For an extended exploration of the importance that the larger liberal tradition attaches to virtue, see Peter Berkowitz, *Virtue and the Making of Modern Liberalism* (Princeton: Princeton University Press, 1999).

Madison's illuminating formulation in *Federalist* No. 10, "a republican remedy for the diseases most incident to republican government."[27]

The Constitution has done more than endure. Well into its third century, the Constitution's experiment in democratic self-government may reasonably be pronounced a remarkable success. Notwithstanding its many imperfections and the daunting challenges it continues to face, the world's oldest liberal democracy remains the freest, most diverse, most prosperous, and mightiest nation the world has ever known. While the balance of interests, policies, and principles it must strike is constantly changing, the need to exercise political moderation in striking the balance remains a paramount political task.

The Federalist*'s Lesson of Moderation*

The Federalist provides unrivaled insight into the Constitution's institutionalization of political moderation. The most famous of its eighty-five papers are probably Nos. 1, 10, 47, 51, 70, and 78. They should serve as a staple of any respectable introduction to American politics and provide a point of departure for any serious renewal of constitutional understanding. Unfortunately, even these deservedly preeminent papers are vanishing from the college curriculum. Rarely is *The Federalist* mandatory reading for the general liberal education of all students, and even political science departments seldom require their students to acquire more than the most cursory knowledge of it.[28] When *The Federalist* is studied,

---

27. *The Federalist*, No. 10, p. 79.

28. See Peter Berkowitz, "Why Colleges Don't Teach *The Federalist Papers*," *The Wall Street Journal*, May 7, 2012, available at http://www.hoover.org/news /daily-report/116621.

its views on the connection between liberty, self-government, and political moderation are generally neglected.

Hamilton introduced the theme of political moderation in *Federalist* No. 1, in the context of an analysis of the difficulties of obtaining an impartial debate about the Constitution's merits. The debate, he stressed, revolved around the momentous question of how the American people should govern themselves. Ratification of the Constitution was necessary to preserve the "existence of the Union, the safety and welfare of the parts of which it is composed, the fate of an empire, in many respects, the most interesting in the world."[29] More was at stake, however, than the future of America:

> It has been frequently remarked that it seems to have been reserved to the people of this country, by their conduct and example, to decide the important question, whether societies of men are really capable or not of establishing good government from reflection and choice, or whether they are forever destined to depend for their political constitutions on accident and force. If there be any truth in the remark, the crisis at which we are arrived may with propriety be regarded as the era in which that decision is to be made; and a wrong election of the part we shall act may, in this view, deserve to be considered as the general misfortune of mankind.[30]

This early assertion of American exceptionalism may appear to brim with immoderation. Yet Hamilton was right: never before had a free and democratic government been established on a continental scale through reflection and choice. His assessment, more-

---

29. *The Federalist*, No. 1, p. 27.
30. Ibid.

over, was neither parochial nor aristocratic; America's crisis of government presented the opportunity to vindicate universal principles of freedom and consent.

Both "patriotism," or love of country, and "philanthropy," or love of humanity, *Federalist* No. 1 states, will impel "all considerate and good men" to consider the significance of the moment and carefully examine the Constitution's merits.[31] In the best case, such men would aspire to "a judicious estimate of our true interests, unperplexed and unbiased by considerations not connected with the public good."[32]

Yet in most cases—even those involving considerate and good men—factors not connected to the public good could be counted on to perplex and bias men's estimates of their true interests. Consequently, genuine deliberation on issues of great political importance was "a thing more ardently to be wished, than seriously to be expected."[33] The extensive political changes embodied in the Constitution compounded the problem: "The plan offered to our deliberations, affects too many particular interests, innovates upon too many local institutions, not to involve in its discussion a variety of objects foreign to its merits, and of views, passions, and prejudices little favourable to the discovery of truth."[34]

Weak or bad men were particularly vulnerable to losing sight of the public interest, but intelligent and public-spirited men were far from immune. Some would resist evaluating the Constitution on the merits because of their vested interest in the old order. Others would seek to foment enmity and division, exploiting disarray by finding profitable opportunities in the breakup of the union.

---

31. Ibid.
32. Ibid.
33. Ibid.
34. Ibid., pp. 27–28.

Still others, acting on the basis of "upright intentions," would oppose change because of "the honest errors of minds led astray by preconceived jealousies and fears." Even the best minds would prove unreliable: "So numerous indeed and so powerful are the causes, which serve to give a false bias to the judgment, that we upon many occasions, see wise and good men on the wrong as well as on the right side of questions, of the first magnitude to society."[35]

The chastening spectacle of bad men rejecting the Constitution for power and profit, and wise and good men failing to grasp its advantages is richly instructive. "If duly attended to," Hamilton observed, the spectacle "would furnish a lesson of moderation to those who are ever so much persuaded of their being in the right in any controversy."[36]

The lesson of moderation that Hamilton gleaned from examination of the abundance of causes that distort judgment and encourage indifference or disdain for the public interest goes well beyond the debate about the Constitution. Rooted in reflections on human nature and freedom, Hamilton's lesson of moderation applies to democratic debate in general, and more broadly to the challenge of designing a government fit for a free people. In politics, our adversaries as well as our allies—and of course we ourselves—are always vulnerable and frequently succumb to impure influences: "Ambition, avarice, personal animosity, party opposition, and many other motives not more laudable than these, are apt to operate as well upon those who support as those who oppose the right side of a question."[37] The knowledge that even those who defend the better alternative—not only in debates about constitutional funda-

---

35. Ibid., p. 28.
36. Ibid. Madison derived a similar lesson in moderation from closely related considerations in *Federalist* No. 37, pp. 220–227.
37. *The Federalist*, No. 1, p. 28.

mentals, but also in controversies over law and public policy—may do so for confused or self-serving reasons counsels patience with the one-sidedness endemic to politics, very much including democratic politics: "Were there not even these inducements to moderation, nothing could be more ill-judged than that intolerant spirit which has, at all times, characterized political parties."[38]

Despite the lesson of, and inducements to, moderation furnished by consideration of the realities of democratic debate, immoderation tends to carry the day. Hamilton suspected that "as in all cases of great national discussion," so too in the debate over the ratification of the Constitution, "a torrent of angry and malignant passions will be let loose" and partisans will seek to win supporters "by the loudness of their declamations, and by the bitterness of their invectives."[39]

In particular, he anticipated that the Constitution's opponents would introduce an invidious distinction between energy in government and protection of the people's liberty.[40] Vigor in rule would be portrayed as a stalking horse for monarchy, and solicitude for the people's rights would be depicted as a calculated bid for "popularity at the expense of the public good."[41] But both energy and liberty are essential features of good government. Indeed, each is essential to the other. To protect against threats to freedom from abroad, a strong and agile government is needed to organize resources, craft strategies, and command forces. To secure rights at home, government also needs strength and agility to enact, implement, and enforce laws. While energy in government can swamp liberty and liberty can sap energy, the proper balance requires ample room for both.

---

38. Ibid., pp. 28–29.
39. Ibid., p. 29.
40. Madison also addressed this theme in *Federalist* No. 37, pp. 220–227.
41. *The Federalist,* No. 1, p. 29.

The reconciliation of enduring political principles is also at issue in Madison's famous analysis of factions in *Federalist* No. 10.[42] A faction is a group of united citizens acting contrary "to the rights of other citizens, or to the permanent and aggregate interests of the community."[43] Factions arise from liberty, are excited and amplified by liberty, and the threat they pose must be dealt with in a manner that respects liberty.

In a society based on natural freedom and equality, the equal protection of individuals' unequal faculties is "the first object of government."[44] Divisions within society spring from the free exercise of unequal faculties, which produces contending interests, most notably the interests connected to the acquisition of different kinds and quantities of property. Unequal acquisition and ownership of property multiplies social divisions by shaping "sentiments and views of the respective proprietors"; these in turn generate "different interests and parties."[45] Madison concluded that "the latent causes of faction are thus sown in the nature of man."[46]

Political freedom amplifies them. What begins with social divisions based on property quickly spreads to religion and politics and eventually extends throughout civil society. Ambitious leaders have perennially "divided mankind into parties, inflamed them with mutual animosity, and rendered them much more disposed to vex and oppress each other than to co-operate for their common good."[47] So central to political life in a free society are parties and factions, and so great a threat do they pose to liberty and stability,

42. *The Federalist,* No. 10, pp. 71–79. See also Hamilton's complementary treatment in *Federalist* No. 9, pp. 66–71.

43. *The Federalist*, No. 10, p. 72.

44. Ibid., p. 73.

45. Ibid.

46. Ibid.

47. Ibid.

that regulating them "forms the principal task of modern legislation."[48]

The unavoidable presence of "the spirit of party and faction" in "the necessary and ordinary operations of the government," however, considerably complicates the task.[49] The presence is unavoidable because citizen legislators are always also interested parties. As creditors or debtors, members of some economic class or another, and taxpayers one and all, lawmakers will always also have private interests in the legislation they debate and on which they vote. Thus the body whose responsibility it is to regulate faction is itself necessarily riven by faction.

Madison did not rule out the possibility of office holders rising above private interest and acting out of devotion to the public good. But because "enlightened statesmen will not always be at the helm," government must be fortified against legislators who fail to harmonize the people's "clashing interests" in light of the public good.[50] Even if enlightened statesmen were at the helm, good government would often remain elusive because it depends on "taking into view indirect and remote considerations, which will rarely prevail over the immediate interest which one party may find in disregarding the rights of another or the good of the whole."[51]

So faction in a free society is unavoidable. Removing its causes is out of the question since that would require regulating opinion or imposing the same interests on each citizen, both of which would destroy the liberty whose preservation is the very purpose of political society. The solution, Madison maintained, consists in controlling factions' effects.

---

48. Ibid., p. 74.
49. Ibid.
50. Ibid., p. 75.
51. Ibid.

Democracies, or democracies traditionally understood, were not well suited to controlling factions' effects. Of course, if the faction was a minority, the majority would defeat the threat to individual rights and the public interest. But in the then-prevailing understanding of democracy, in which citizens met directly to decide matters of law and policy, there was no cure for majority faction—or what John Stuart Mill would later call "the tyranny of the majority"[52]—consistent with the preservation of freedom. This was a fatal flaw since all experience showed that when given the opportunity, majorities had been quick to implement "schemes of oppression" and "neither religious nor moral motives can be relied on as an adequate control."[53] Hence, democracies "have ever been spectacles of turbulence and contention; have ever been found incompatible with personal security, or the rights of property; and have in general been as short in their lives, as they have been violent in their deaths."[54] Because of their internal structure—or lack of it—direct or pure democracies fail to combine liberty with stability, and so destroy both.

One of the improvements that would enable the Constitution, consistent with the principles of republican self-government, to control the destabilizing effects of faction was the institution of representation, or delegation of the tasks of government to a small number of citizens elected by the rest. Representation creates the opportunity "to refine and enlarge the public views" by placing responsibility for lawmaking in the hands of those "whose wisdom may best discern the true interest of their country, and whose

52. John Stuart Mill, *On Liberty,* in *J.S. Mill and Other Writings,* ed. Stefan Collini (Cambridge: Cambridge University Press, 1989), p. 8.

53. *The Federalist,* No. 10, p. 75.

54. Ibid., p. 76.

patriotism and love of justice, will be least likely to sacrifice it to temporary or partial considerations."[55]

Since even the least likely to neglect the public interest are fallible, the scheme of representation must be carefully calibrated. Citizens will not always choose representatives wisely and representatives will not always perform their tasks responsibly. Accordingly, there must be enough representatives "to guard against the cabals of the few" but not so many as to unleash "the confusion of a multitude."[56] At the same time, care must be given so that electoral districts do not become so large that representatives grow remote from "local circumstances and lesser interests."[57] Nor should representatives be elected by so few that preoccupation with the local and lesser renders them unfit to "comprehend and pursue great and national objects."[58]

The second improvement for dealing with the effects of faction involved increasing the number of citizens and enlarging the country's territory. Traditionally, republics were small by definition, the size of a city. Madison argued that small size was a principal cause of their instability because it allowed for a majority faction to dominate, or a few minority factions to undermine the state. In contrast, a larger territory and population multiplies "the variety

---

55. Ibid. So too had Burke argued in 1774, in his "Speech to the Electors of Bristol," in *The Works of the Right Honourable Edmund Burke,* Vol. II (London: John C. Nimmo, 1887), available at http://www.gutenberg.org/files/15198/15198-h/15198-h.htm#ELECTORS_OF_BRISTOL.

56. *The Federalist,* No. 10, p. 77.

57. Ibid.

58. Ibid. For more on the considerations that must be balanced in determining the size of the most representative part of the federal government, the House of Representatives, see *Federalist* No. 55, pp. 338–343, and *Federalist* No. 56, pp. 343–347.

of parties and interests," dispersing citizens' energies and increasing the number of associations that have some claim on them, thereby reducing the likelihood that a majority faction will arise to trample on the rights of minorities or that a few factions will disrupt or paralyze the people.[59] The constant clash and competition of many and varied interests characteristic of liberal democracy in America today, a reflection of constitutional design, may not always be edifying or inspiring. But by thwarting the rise of a single overweening majority or the emergence of a few powerful minorities hostile to the public interest, the multiplication of parties and interests provides a vital safeguard of freedom.[60]

The Constitution's separation of powers scheme also exemplifies the institutionalization of political moderation. Distinguishing the legislative, executive, and judicial functions of government by giving to each its own department was "an essential precaution in favor of liberty," as Madison argued in *Federalist* No. 47.[61] So the distinct powers of government can work together effectively, the Constitution also blends them, giving each branch a small but significant share in the work of the others.[62] The legislative branch, for example, must confirm federal judges and has the power to impeach the president and remove him from office; the president

---

59. *The Federalist,* No. 10, p. 78.

60. To the argument that the extensive republic created by the Constitution would be too large and powerful to preserve republican principles, *The Federalist* replies that the smaller confederacies of a limited number of states that had been considered as an alternative to a union of all the states would still require a government as comprehensive as the one proposed by the Constitution. Indeed, even the states themselves were vastly larger than classical republican theory contemplated and were of a size that would call for "the same energy of government, and the same forms of administration" incorporated in the Constitution. See *The Federalist,* No. 13, pp. 92–94, and No. 14, pp. 94–100.

61. *The Federalist,* No. 47, p. 297.

62. *The Federalist,* No. 48, pp. 305–310.

signs and vetoes legislation and appoints judges; and the judiciary can strike down congressional statutes and declare presidential actions unconstitutional.

During the ratifying debates, this blending looked to many critics like a gross violation of the separation of powers. To the contrary, argued Madison, it was fully consistent with that "sacred maxim of free government," provided that the maxim was well understood.[63] The limited blending of separate and distinct powers comported with the common practice of state governments in America. And it reflected the political teaching of the "celebrated Montesquieu,"[64] which all sides agreed was authoritative. Montesquieu, Madison emphasized, did not require that each branch be pure, but rather that no two principal functions of government be combined entirely in a single branch.

To keep the separate powers separate, however, the Constitution does not rely only or ultimately on "parchment barriers."[65] Rather, it is structured to prudently channel passions and interests. As Madison explained in *Federalist* No. 51, the Constitution organizes the legislative, executive, and judicial branches so that in advancing their interests and performing their constitutional tasks, office holders also will serve as "the means of keeping each other in their proper places."[66] Assuming that the passions and interests that impel men to compete for high office are usually impure and will continue to exert their influence once men attain high office, the Constitution adopts a "policy of supplying by opposite and rival interests, the defect of better motives."[67] The policy is implemented through "inventions of prudence"—constitutional structures in

---

63. *The Federalist,* No. 47, p. 304.
64. Ibid., p. 298.
65. *The Federalist,* No. 48, p. 305.
66. *The Federalist,* No. 51, p. 318.
67. Ibid., p. 319.

which "ambition must be made to counteract ambition" and that equip members of each of the three branches with powers to resist encroachment by the others.[68] By aligning office holders' personal pride in publicly recognized achievement with the rights and prerogatives of their office, the Constitution seeks to harness powerful passions and interests and place them in the service of the public good. Without relying overly much on virtue—and without denying its necessity either—the Constitution aims at improving the chances for legislation consistent with the requirements of the public good by giving office holders in each branch a private interest in checking the propensity to overreach common to all.

So critical is the structure of government to the protection of freedom that Hamilton argued in *Federalist* No. 84 that a bill of rights would not only be superfluous but counterproductive.[69] As Madison stressed in *Federalist* No. 45, the Constitution forms a government of limited and enumerated powers: "The powers delegated by the proposed Constitution to the federal government are few and defined. Those which are to remain in the State governments are numerous and indefinite."[70] There was no need to prohibit the federal government from, for example, infringing on the rights of religion and speech, because it had no powers with which to do so. Furthermore, argued Hamilton, expressly prohibiting the federal government from exercising powers it did not possess was dangerous because it might give rise to the destabilizing inference that the federal government possessed unenumerated powers.

Still, the Constitution's complex institutional arrangements as well as its first ten amendments—the Bill of Rights, which despite Hamilton's objections came into effect in 1791—

---

68. Ibid.
69. *The Federalist,* No. 84, pp. 509–515.
70. *The Federalist,* No. 45, p. 289.

were at best "auxiliary precautions."[71] The ultimate precaution was a "dependence on the people."[72] All parts of government ultimately must answer through elections to the people, who are the original source of legitimate political power—even judges are appointed and confirmed by elected representatives.[73] The ultimate dependence on the people did not change the vital importance of well-designed institutions. Accordingly, Madison observed in *Federalist* No. 51 that since men are not angels and angels do not govern men, the structure of political institutions must operate first to enable the government to control the governed and then to oblige government to control itself.[74] At the same time, as Madison noted in *Federalist* No. 55, because constitutional democracy depends on the consent of the people—which calls on their judgment, vigilance, and love of liberty—it relies on virtue to a greater degree than any other form of government.[75]

Despite the Constitution's auxiliary and ultimate precautions, Anti-Federalists condemned the executive, which they saw as a poorly disguised monarch, and attacked the federal judiciary capped by the Supreme Court, which they believed was vested with the anti-democratic power to strike down acts of Congress the justices found to conflict with the Constitution. Hamilton defended both, showing that the institutions were designed to achieve the proper balance, securing liberty while operating within the constraints imposed by republican principles.

---

71. *The Federalist*, No. 51, p. 319.

72. Ibid.

73. For reiterations of the conviction that the ultimate precaution against governmental abuse of power is dependence on the people, see, for example, *The Federalist*, No. 21, pp. 134–139; No. 22, pp. 139–148; No. 33, pp. 197–201; No. 44, pp. 277–284; No. 46, pp. 290–297; No. 49, pp. 310–314; and No. 57, pp. 348–353.

74. *The Federalist*, No. 51, p. 319.

75. *The Federalist*, No. 55, p. 343.

In *Federalist* No. 70, Hamilton argued that energy in the executive is crucial to defending the nation against foreign threats, administering the laws, and protecting individual rights.[76] Placing the executive power in one person—however large the branch he directs may grow—was the most effective means of ensuring that the president would be able to act vigorously, promptly and, where necessary, with secrecy. These features of executive power suggest conduct characteristic of a monarch. But the executive was not placed above the law. Hamilton insisted, moreover, that the countervailing forces built into the Constitution would keep the president in check, while enabling him to use his monarch-like powers to defend the nation, enforce the law, and protect rights. In addition, the people would be better able to hold a unitary executive responsible and to remove him within four years through an election, or sooner if the House impeached him and the Senate found him guilty of "high crimes and misdemeanors." So successful has the Constitution been in anchoring the executive in the will of the people that presidential elections, the only elections in the country in which all eligible voters have the opportunity to participate, have come to be seen as the apex of American democracy.

Similarly, in *Federalist* No. 78, Hamilton maintained that despite the appearance of a threat to democratic legitimacy, the federal judiciary advances the cause of freedom by combining independence and accountability.[77] To obtain the requisite integrity and impartiality, the Constitution reduces the role of electoral politics in forming the federal judiciary by relying on presidential nomination and Senate confirmation. In addition, the Constitution confers life tenure on judges on condition of good behavior. This frees judges from dependence on regular reconsideration by

---

76. *The Federalist*, No. 70, pp. 421–429.
77. *The Federalist*, No. 78, pp. 463–471.

the political branches and the people. The independence of the courts is necessary because their job is to master the complex body of law that naturally develops in a free society and, in the form of reasoned and impartial decisions, apply it to the cases and controversies that come before them. At the same time, the judiciary's dependence on the political branches, though attenuated, is necessary and desirable because all exercises of power in a republic must be derived from the consent of the governed.

The Constitution does not explicitly provide for what has come to be called judicial review—the power to strike down legislation and invalidate acts of the executive as inconsistent with the Constitution. Nor does Hamilton use the term. But he does insist that the Constitution's structure reasonably gives rise to the presumption that an essential part of the federal judiciary's job is to keep the people's representatives within limits assigned by the Constitution. After all, "the interpretation of the laws is the proper and peculiar province of the courts"[78] and, as Article VI, Clause 2, proclaims, the Constitution is the supreme law of the land, along with the treaties and U.S. laws made pursuant to it. Moreover, judicial review is rooted in the idea of consent. When the judiciary strikes down as inconsistent with the Constitution a law passed by Congress and signed by the president, it invalidates the will of a temporary and passing majority in the name of the people's most deeply considered and most fundamental legal judgments, which are inscribed in the Constitution.[79] To the objection that judicial review elevates the judiciary above the other branches, Hamilton famously replied that the judiciary is the "least dangerous" of the branches because it lacks the power of the purse, which

---

78. Ibid., p. 466.
79. Ibid.

is assigned to Congress, and the power of the sword, which is assigned to the executive.[80]

Looking back over the last seventy years, these reassurances may seem quaint given the range of divisive questions the Supreme Court has decided. Yet the people continue to retain ultimate responsibility for securing liberty. They may elect a president and a Congress that, consistent with a reasonable reading of the Constitution, will repeal laws the Court declined to overturn or elect representatives who will enact requirements that the Court refused to mandate. Or the people can elect a president who will appoint and Senators who will confirm justices with judicial philosophies more in keeping with their opinions about the role of judges in a liberal democracy. And the people are always at liberty to amend the Constitution in accordance with procedures spelled out in Article V. These undertakings are certainly not made easy by the Constitution. But the difficulty of altering the legal judgments of the most politically insulated of the three branches reflects the Constitution's institutionalization of political moderation.

In *Federalist* No. 85, Hamilton closed the series of articles in behalf of ratification by returning to the theme of moderation with which he began. With eleven of thirteen states having ratified the Constitution since the publication of *Federalist* No. 1 and having thereby established it among themselves (in accordance with Article VII), he argued against those who wanted to make changes to it before it was "irrevocably established."[81] That would require beginning the arduous ratification process all over again. As Benjamin Franklin had declared on the final day of the Convention[82]

---

80. Ibid., p. 464.

81. *The Federalist,* No. 85, p. 523.

82. Benjamin Franklin, speech of Sept. 17, 1787, available at http://avalon. law.yale.edu/18th_century/debates_917.asp.

and as Madison had argued in *Federalist* No. 37,[83] though imperfect, the Constitution "is the best that the present views and circumstances of the country will permit; and is such a one as promises every species of security which a reasonable people can desire."[84]

In quoting the "judicious reflections" of Scottish philosopher David Hume, Hamilton offered an apt statement of the limits of constitution-making for an extended polity:

> "To balance a large state or society [says he], whether monarchical or republican, on general laws, is a work of so great difficulty, that no human genius, however comprehensive, is able, by the mere dint of reason and reflection, to effect it. The judgments of many must unite in the work; experience must guide their labor; time must bring it to perfection, and the feeling of inconveniences must correct the mistakes which they INEVITABLY fall into in their first trials and experiments."[85]

Hamilton went on to assert that Hume's words about the difficulty of achieving a correct initial balance in forming a constitution and the necessity of constantly rebalancing as prudence dictates

> contain a lesson of moderation to all the sincere lovers of the Union, and ought to put them upon their guard against hazarding anarchy, civil war, a perpetual alienation of the States from each other, and perhaps the military despotism of a victorious demagogue, in the pursuit of what they are not likely to obtain, but from TIME AND EXPERIENCE.[86]

---

83. *The Federalist*, No. 37, pp. 220–227.
84. *The Federalist*, No. 85, p. 523.
85. Ibid., p. 526.
86. Ibid.

Hamilton's lesson of moderation does not counsel resigned acceptance of the Constitution's imperfections but rather determination to improve the union within the sturdy framework of liberty that the Constitution establishes.

The Anti-Federalists were not convinced. They argued that the Constitution failed disastrously to achieve a balance that supported liberty. In their view, the constitutional scheme of representation would inevitably prove unrepresentative, producing distant and out-of-touch legislators. They charged that Article I's "necessary and proper clause"[87] would allow the federal government to impose unfair and destructive taxes and regulation and swallow up state governments. And they contended that with its sweeping powers of review the federal judiciary would crush state judiciaries. The Constitution, the Anti-Federalists warned, would strangle liberty in its cradle.

The extraordinary reply to the Anti-Federalists' critique of the Constitution contained in the eighty-five essays comprising *The Federalist* attests to the salience of Anti-Federalist concerns at the time of ratification. And the persistence for two centuries of robust debate about the quality of representation, the allocation of power between the federal and state governments, and the extent of legitimate judicial power under the Constitution attests to the salience of their concerns today.

This would not have shocked the authors of *The Federalist.* The framers' understanding of the unceasing need in the politics of a free society to adjust and readjust, balance and rebalance, cali-

---

87. "The Congress shall have Power . . . To make all Laws which shall be necessary and proper for carrying into Execution the foregoing Powers and all other Powers vested by this Constitution in the Government of the United States, or in any Department or Officer thereof." United States Constitution, Article I, Section 8.

brate and recalibrate impelled them to craft a durable and flexible arrangement of political institutions for conducting the work of government and for debating the work of government. *The Federalist* reinforces the lesson of moderation inscribed in the Constitution it expounds and defends.

The Constitution and the Paradox of Freedom

On October 6, 1787, at the Pennsylvania State House—known today as Independence Hall—James Wilson, who signed the Declaration of Independence and played a major role at the Constitutional Convention, delivered an early and influential speech in support of the ratification. Launching the campaign for ratification three weeks before Hamilton published the first installment of *The Federalist*, Wilson stressed that vested interests would generate powerful opposition to the new scheme of government. Like Franklin, Madison, and Hamilton, Wilson acknowledged that because of necessary compromises, the Constitution did not attain perfection. And, like the *The Federalist*, he drew from the struggle to frame the Constitution a lesson of, and inducements to, moderation:

> when I reflect how widely men differ in their opinions, and that every man (and the observation applies likewise to every State) has an equal pretension to assert his own, I am satisfied that anything nearer to perfection could not have been accomplished. If there are errors, it should be remembered that the seeds of reformation are sown in the work itself and the concurrence of two-thirds of the Congress may at any time introduce alterations and amendments. Regarding it, then, in every point of view, with a candid and disinterested mind, I am bold to

assert that it is the best form of government which has ever been offered to the world.[88]

Wilson's measured boldness, in keeping with the spirit that pervades *The Federalist,* suggests that it takes political moderation to appreciate the Constitution's institutionalization of political moderation. It also takes political moderation to appreciate the Constitution's incompleteness and unfinished work. One of the diseases incident to republican government for which the Constitution does not provide a cure is the enervation of political moderation by the achievement of freedom.

As I observed in chapter 2, it is a paradox of freedom that the more one has, the more one wants. Freedom disposes individuals to bristle at authority, to incline toward novelty, and to make their own rules. By expanding choice and producing abundance and affluence, free political institutions and free markets amplify these dispositions. Consequently, the enjoyment of freedom's blessings tends to foster impatience with the political order that enables free citizens to cooperate and compete, and to weaken interest in cultivating, exercising, and transmitting the virtues required for prospering in private and public life. Progress in freedom compounds the challenge of achieving that reasonable balance between liberty and restraint that the framers of the Constitution, very much in agreement with Burke, taught was vital.

Thus, progress in freedom, of the sort the American political tradition has amply exhibited, makes the conservative task more urgent and more complex. While conservatives' electoral fortunes in the United States may wax and wane, progress in freedom steadily increases the need for a constitutional conservatism that

---

88. James Wilson speech, available at http://www.lexrex.com/enlightened /writings/jwilson.htm.

preserves liberty by keeping government limited and by giving tradition, order, and virtue their due. Because liberty depends on a variety of principles, balancing those principles must remain critical to the conservation and correction of liberty. Indeed, recognition that the balance of liberty with tradition, order, and virtue within the American system of limited government has been upset is a defining feature of the distinctive form of American conservatism that arose in the 1940s and 1950s, culminated in the presidency of Ronald Reagan, and lost its way during the George W. Bush years.

CHAPTER 4

Constitutional Conservatism in America: *Recovering Liberty*

American conservatism became conscious of itself as a distinctive school in the years following World War II. Its libertarian strand was powerfully put forward in the mid-1940s in Friedrich August Hayek's *The Road to Serfdom* and the social conservative strand received forceful expression in the early 1950s in Russell Kirk's *The Conservative Mind* and Whittaker Chamber's *Witness*. These competing strands were vigorously debated in the pages of *National Review* in the second half of the 1950s, and strikingly synthesized by Frank S. Meyer in the early 1960s. Conservatism was unveiled to the larger public in Barry Goldwater's ill-fated run for president in 1964; reached a culmination in the 1980s in the seminal presidency of Ronald Reagan; splintered in the late 1990s following Representative Newt Gingrich's rise and fall; found itself even more sharply divided and demoralized in 2009 as George W. Bush left office; and discovered renewed purpose and vigor in response to President Barack Obama's determination to accomplish a progressive transformation of America.

With Mitt Romney's close loss to President Obama in November 2012 even as Republicans extended their 2010 gains in state legislatures and governorships, American conservatism stands at a crossroads. In moving forward, it would do well to study the high points of American conservatism over the last seventy years, which confirm Burke's teaching that the conservation and correction of liberty depend on reconciling liberty with tradition, order, and virtue.[1]

Of course there had always been conservatives in America. Russell Kirk, a father of traditionalist conservatism, showed this in 1953 in *The Conservative Mind: From Burke to Eliot,* itself a major contribution to the post–World War II renaissance in conservative thinking. Kirk argued that "the essence of social conservatism is preservation of the ancient moral traditions of humanity."[2] Conservatives worthy of the name, he contended, bring to their task a common set of convictions: belief in a transcendent moral order; appreciation of the variety of human types and ways of life; respect for social order and hierarchies; grasp of the close link between individual freedom and the protection of private property; preference for the wisdom embodied in custom and convention, combined with distrust of moralists and social scientists seeking to reconstruct society on the basis of grand theories; and understanding of both liberal democracy's dangerous attraction to hasty innovation and its perennial need for prudent reform.[3] Accordingly, social conservatism in America contains within itself the tension between liberty on the one hand and tradition, order, and virtue on the other as it embraces both the idea that inherited beliefs and practices reflect an authoritative moral order and the idea that government must be limited for the sake of freedom,

---

1. For an illuminating and detailed exploration of post–World War II American conservatism, see George H. Nash, *The Conservative Intellectual Movement in America since 1945,* 2nd ed. (Wilmington, Del.: Intercollegiate Studies Institute, 2006). For a lucid overview stretching back to the founding, see Patrick Allitt, *The Conservatives: Ideas and Personalities Throughout American History* (New Haven, Conn.: Yale University Press, 2009).

2. Russell Kirk, *The Conservative Mind: From Burke to Eliot,* 7th rev. ed. (Lake Bluff, Ill.: Regnery, 1986, orig. 1953), p. 8.

3. Ibid., pp. 8–9.

with high priority given to economic freedom. One can see elements of conservatism so understood at work, Kirk demonstrated, in the careers and ideas of, among others, John Adams, Alexander Hamilton, John Randolph, John C. Calhoun, James Fenimore Cooper, John Quincy Adams, Orestes Brownson, Nathaniel Hawthorne, James Russell Lowell, Henry Adams, Brooke Adams, Irving Babbitt, Paul Elmer Moore, George Santayana, and T.S. Eliot. Although none made the meaning of conservatism in America a guiding theme of his work, Kirk's distillation of their views in *The Conservative Mind* helped set the stage for those who would, including Kirk himself.

The post–World War II entrenchment of the New Deal and the rise of communism combined to jolt a self-consciously conservative movement in America into existence. The libertarian strand sought to combat the New Deal's expansion of the size, scope, and responsibilities of the federal government and the collectivist temptation embodied in Soviet communism. The single most influential analysis of the great threat to liberty presented by both came from outside of the United States in the form of Friedrich A. Hayek's *The Road to Serfdom*. The book first appeared in Great Britain in 1944, and became a bestseller in the United States thanks in part to the publication in 1945 of an abridged version in *Reader's Digest*.

Born in Austria-Hungary in 1899 and a professor at the London School of Economics from 1938 to 1950 before moving to the University of Chicago, Hayek saw himself as an heir to the classical liberal tradition. That tradition, which embraces Burke and *The Federalist*, flourished in the late-eighteenth and nineteenth centuries, particularly in Great Britain and the United States. It declared that the leading aim of politics was to secure individual liberty. It stressed that limiting government's scope and dispersing government's power were critical to securing liberty. And it highlighted the dependence of political freedom on economic freedom. In accordance with that tradition, Hayek's target was not, as many suppose, any and all government regulation of the economy. Rather, as he stressed throughout *The Road to Serfdom*, it was central planning, in which government assumed primary responsibility for decisions about production and distribution.

In the 1962 bestseller *Capitalism and Freedom,* Hayek's University of Chicago colleague Milton Friedman expounded views similar to those of Hayek. Friedman favored severely scaling back government involvement in the economy and applied free market principles to a range of public policy issues including the draft, education, and poverty. He regretted that the opponents of the political tradition he championed, who by the 1960s had come to dominate the universities and elite opinion, had appropriated the term "liberalism."[4] He not only declared that conservatism "was not a satisfactory alternative" as a label for his own views, but went so far as to insist on "using the word liberalism in its original sense—as the doctrines pertaining to a free man."[5]

Hayek, too, found the description of his work as conservative unsatisfactory. With a view to its European variants, he associated conservatism with a defense of monarchy and the political authority of religion, nationalism, a transcendent and authoritative moral order, and paternalistic government.[6] Despite his reservations, it is fitting that he described his task in conservative terms. According to the foreword to the 1956 American paperback edition of *The Road to Serfdom,* the task was "the preservation of a free

---

4. Milton Friedman, *Capitalism and Freedom* (Chicago: University of Chicago Press, 1982, orig. 1962), p. 4.

5. Ibid., p. 6.

6. See Hayek's postcript, "Why I Am Not a Conservative," *The Constitution of Liberty* (Chicago: University of Chicago Press, 1960), pp. 397–414.

society."[7] Hayek's description applies to Friedman and implies a Burkean corollary: the reform of existing institutions in light of the teachings of the classical liberal tradition involves a disposition to preserve and depends on an ability to improve.[8]

Threats to freedom from abroad especially stirred conservative instincts and focused conservative thought. The Allied victory over Nazi totalitarianism in World War II was swiftly followed by the emergence of communist totalitarianism in the form of the Soviet Union as the great rival to the United States, and the onset of the Cold War between the two superpowers. Communism rejected individual rights, subordinated the individual to the state, centralized control over the economy in the government, presented an alternative to liberal democracy that held mass appeal, and sought to extend its worldwide reach through conquest and subjugation.

No book offered a more penetrating account of communism as "the focus of the concentrated evil of our time" than *Witness,* by Whittaker Chambers.[9] A former member of the Communist Party, Chambers had earned the enmity of left-liberal intellectual and political elites for his testimony in the perjury and espionage trial of Alger Hiss. Chambers's monumental memoir of his journey from communism to the principles of freedom and Christian faith eloquently and uncompromisingly argues that the contest between communism and freedom culminates with the choice between an amoral world of false freedom in which man degrades himself by seeking to become absolutely sovereign, and a moral

---

7. F.A. Hayek, *The Road to Serfdom* (Chicago: University of Chicago, 2007, orig. 1944), p. 44.

8. See Edmund Burke, *Reflections on the Revolution in France,* in *The Works of the Right Honourable Edmund Burke,* Vol. III (London: John C. Nimmo, 1887), p. 440; see also pp. 455–460, available at http://www.gutenberg.org /files/15679/15679-h/15679-h.htm#REFLECTIONS.

9. Whittaker Chambers, *Witness* (Washington, D.C.: Regnery, 1987, orig. 1952), p. 8.

world of true freedom in which man recognizes the soul's dignity under God's sovereignty.

To fight the collectivist impulse at home and abroad, many followed Kirk and Chambers and sought to conserve freedom by restoring traditional morality and faith. Others followed Hayek and Friedman and undertook to conserve freedom through a restoration of classical liberalism, which rigorously limited the state and came to be called libertarianism. But what emerged as the dominant strand in modern American conservatism set out to conserve freedom by restoring both.

William F. Buckley Jr., the most influential voice of conservatism over the last seventy years, took the lead in fashioning a political orientation that combined a dedication to traditional morality and faith with a devotion to liberty, particularly religious and economic liberty. Conservatism's flagship publication, *National Review*—which Buckley founded in 1955, served as editor-in-chief of until 1990, and to which he contributed until his death in 2008—was the leading vehicle. And the most influential conservative politicians during that period—Barry Goldwater, Ronald Reagan, Newt Gingrich, and George W. Bush—all sought with varying degrees of success to blend social conservative and libertarian elements. Despite its stumbles and falls, American conservatism's quest after World War II to combine and balance diverse political principles provides a lesson of political moderation.

Conservatism in America has not always been guided by political moderation. Some conservative thinkers and office holders overlooked the tensions between individual liberty and traditional morality. Others chose one and insisted that the other was entirely antagonistic. Sometimes conservatives gave too much weight to the claims of stability and too little to the need for reform. Sometimes they were late to appreciate shifting tides of public opinion and popular sentiment. Sometimes they conceived of themselves as revolutionaries, committed to returning to or re-creating forms of life that had little resonance with contemporary American majorities. Sometimes they fought futile rearguard actions confusing the imperative to limit government with delusory aspirations to shrink it to its eighteenth-century size. Nevertheless, by affirming that the fate of liberty and tradition were inextricably intertwined, the dominant strand of American conservatism yields a lesson of political moderation, even on occasion in its characteristic excesses.

Buckley prominently displayed that affirmation in 1951 in his first book, *God & Man at Yale,* though the lesson of moderation it yields was not what first impressed readers, be they delighted allies or enraged critics. He argued that his alma mater had deeply embedded in the university curriculum a dogmatic atheism and collectivistic ideology that had become invisible to faculty and administrators because they so thoroughly and thoughtlessly subscribed to it. The book made the 24-year-old Buckley a national sensation and, among the intellectuals, notorious. It also launched the modern conservative movement.

The preface forthrightly announces Buckley's devotion to traditional religious faith and economic and political liberty:

> I had always been taught, and experience had fortified the teachings, that an active faith in God and a rigid adherence to Christian principles are the most powerful influences toward the good life. I also believed, with only a scanty knowledge of economics, that free enterprise and limited government had served this country well and would probably continue to do so in the future.[10]

---

10. William F. Buckley Jr., *God & Man at Yale* (Washington, D.C.: Regnery, 2001, orig. 1951), p. lxiii.

Buckley's critique of academic orthodoxy at Yale was all the more powerful—and all the more baffling to that orthodoxy's guardians—for its defense of freedom. How could one who condemned the relentless atheism of the curriculum, who argued for the importance of the study of religion in general, and who insisted on Yale's obligation to sympathetically expound the teachings of Christianity be anything but a religious reactionary?

And how could one who found in the Yale economics and political science departments a dogmatic commitment to collectivism; who discerned in the devotion to Keynes and in the omission from the curriculum of Hayek and Hayek's mentor, the Austrian economist Ludwig von Mises, evidence of spectacular one-sidedness; and who believed that Yale had an obligation to teach appreciation of the achievements of capitalism and limited government, be seen as other than an apologist for fat cats, an enemy of progress, and hostile to the needs of the human spirit?

Buckley further offended faculty and administration sensibilities by insisting that alumni should play a major role in academic affairs, envisaging them, in accordance with their official responsibilities, as "ultimate overseers of Yale's educational policy."[11] According to Buckley, Yale alumni—who then, as today, footed a good deal of the cost of Yale—had the right, the power, and the duty to ensure that Yale lived up to liberal education's proper goals.

Buckley knew that for his criticisms of Yale and proposals for reform he would be accused of ignorance of or disdain for academic freedom. His powerful reply remains powerful today. A "laissez-faire education" that allowed professors to teach whatever they wished and students to study whatever they wanted represented an abdication of responsibility by Yale and a repudiation of

---

11. Ibid., p. 122.

standards.[12] And the inculcation of secular and progressive values under the guise of the openness to all ideas constituted educational fraud.

Academic freedom did not give professors license to pontificate as they pleased in the classroom, in Buckley's view, but rather provided liberty to pursue the truth and to prepare students for the challenges of freedom. The pillars of freedom in America, he maintained, were the free market economy, which encouraged industriousness and self-reliance by protecting private property, and Christianity, which provided the only secure foundation for belief in the dignity of the individual. Of course, Buckley argued, liberal education also included study of the limitations and defects of free peoples and free societies.

The young Buckley worried that if alumni in his time did not take action to reform the university, the next generation of alumni would be so thoroughly imbued with illiberal and anti-religious attitudes that they would lose an understanding of the purpose of liberal education and become blind to the urgent need to reform Yale. Reform was urgent because Yale's betrayal of liberal education's mission to pursue truth and educate for freedom had civic consequences: it deprived students of that capstone to their formal studies that enabled them to exercise their rights most effectively and discharge their duties wisely. And in depriving its students, Yale deprived the nation of a genuinely educated elite.

A prodigiously productive career spanning nearly sixty years followed Buckley's dramatic national debut. In addition to his work as *National Review*'s editor-in-chief, he wrote three newspaper columns a week for several decades, lectured around the country for roughly two months a year, wrote more than fifty books, and from the mid-1960s to the late-1990s hosted *Firing Line,* an

---

12. Ibid., p. 126.

erudite and entertaining television show devoted to the debate of political ideas and public policy.

The "Credenda and Statement of Principles" that appeared in 1955 in the first issue of *National Review* cheerfully exhibited Buckley's commitment to both individual liberty and traditional morality.[13] Setting his undertaking against the intellectual hegemony of left-liberalism and the conformity of thought in general and the prejudice in favor of moral relativism that it spawned in particular, Buckley proclaimed that to secure freedom, the growth of government "must be fought relentlessly." He declared that politics must be adjusted to account for the truths of human nature and the transcendent truths of traditional morality. Human nature could not, as the left sought, be refashioned to make it compatible with utopian schemes. Communism, "the century's most blatant force of Satanic utopianism," needed to be not merely contained but defeated. The liberal hold on high and popular culture had to be resisted in the name of excellence and informed dissent. Liberal efforts to transform both parties into bearers of progressive pieties also had to be opposed. Instead, conservatives would have to insist on a two-party system in which one of the parties would be genuinely conservative and would champion the idea that a free market economy not only promotes material prosperity but also political freedom. And because political centralization and remote government threaten freedom, conservatives were duty-bound to reject categorically the progressive dream of world government.

While apparently effortless for Buckley, the simultaneous devotion to individual liberty and traditional morality could not be seen in each and every one of the journalists, scholars, publi-

---

13. William F. Buckley Jr., "Credenda and Statement of Principles," in *Conservatism in America since 1930,* ed. Gregory L. Schneider (New York: New York University Press, 2003), pp. 200–205; also available at http://www.national review.com/articles/223549/our-mission-statement/william-f-buckley-jr.

cists, and polemicists who graced *National Review*'s pages over the decades. Some libertarian contributors did not cease to regard social conservatives as reactionaries, and some social conservatives did not abandon the conviction that libertarians were shallow and decadent. Nevertheless, by providing a forum in which social conservatives and libertarian conservatives could vigorously air their disagreements, Buckley's magazine sent a message that both were original and indispensable members of the same intellectual and political family devoted to preserving freedom, and that hospitality to both was a conservative imperative.

Buckley's was an "enlightened conservatism," in Roger Kimball's provocative phrase.[14] Much like the political ideas of Burke and *The Federalist,* the Buckley brand of conservatism presupposes the Enlightenment's leading moral and political principles, not in the sense of philosophizing based on them, but of accepting them with gratitude. Indeed, Buckley's conservatism admires people with independent minds who take responsibility for themselves and their families. And it embraces a politics devoted to individual freedom.

But Buckley's conservatism is also enlightened in a more complex and less orthodox sense. Much like Burke's critique of the French Revolution, Buckley's conservatism exposes Enlightenment excesses, particularly Enlightenment thinking's unreasonable reliance on abstract reasoning about morals and politics, and dogmatic disparagement of the wisdom acquired through experience and embodied in traditional practices and institutions.

Not that one finds in Buckley's writings much in the way of speculative thought or philosophical critique proper. The effort to sort out the theoretical tensions between liberty and tradition did

---

14. Introduction, William F. Buckley Jr., *Athwart History: Half a Century of Polemics, Animadversions, and Illuminations: A William F. Buckley Jr. Omnibus,* eds. Linda Bridges and Roger Kimball (New York: Encounter Books, 2010), p. xxviii.

not much command his interest. But in examining the blessings of liberty, the hubris of the left, the intricacies of public policy, the evils of communism, the pleasures of music, the rewards of friendship and family, and the consolations of religion Buckley brilliantly demonstrated how liberty and tradition can in practice cheerfully and proudly coexist. Appreciating the texture of that coexistence is, from the Buckley point of view, a rational imperative.

Finally, Buckley's conservatism is enlightened in the sense that it self-consciously considers what is worthy in tradition and deserving of conservation. In its simplest form, conservatism seeks to preserve inherited moral and religious beliefs and to transmit them to the next generation. But Buckley's conservatism confronts a more daunting task. At its core, the American inheritance involves a devotion to freedom and the fundamental beliefs, practices, and institutions on which freedom rests. But, as I have observed in connection with Burke and *The Federalist,* freedom generates distrust of tradition, impatience with order, and depreciation of virtue, thereby encouraging habits of heart and mind that threaten the conditions that sustain freedom. In his life, Buckley exuberantly combined liberty and tradition, and in his writings he reconciled them not by means of philosophical argument but by rendering moral and political judgments that embody due respect for both.

In his 1962 book *In Defense of Freedom: A Conservative Credo,* Frank S. Meyer confronted the clash between traditionalists and libertarians head on, and provided what remains today among the most clear and compelling reconciliations of their competing conservatisms. A senior editor and columnist at *National Review* from 1957 until his death in 1972, Meyer aimed "to vindicate the freedom of the person as the central and primary end of political society."[15] Crucial to this vindication was showing that a politics

---

15. Frank S. Meyer, *In Defense of Freedom: A Conservative Credo,* in *In Defense of Freedom and Related Essays* (Indianapolis: Liberty Fund, 1962), p. 33.

that put freedom first was not only consistent with but inseparable from conservative assumptions about an objective, abiding, and authoritative moral order. Also crucial was his claim that the synthesis of liberty and tradition that he sought to vindicate on a theoretical plane was embodied in the Declaration of Independence, the Constitution, the ratifying debates, and, indeed, in the common-sense opinions and attitudes of contemporary American conservatives. In other words, the primacy of individual freedom and the indispensableness of tradition flow from both the moral principles to which conservatives are philosophically committed and from fidelity to fundamental features of the American political tradition.

In Meyer's view, the two great schools of the post–World War II conservative renewal each contained a crucial truth and each took a wrong turn. In the nineteenth century, classical liberalism embraced utilitarianism, which measured policy by the capacity to promote the greatest good for the greatest number. By elevating the collective good and setting aside the idea of individual rights, this Benthamite doctrine, Meyer argued, undermined the idea that each human being is an end himself, an idea that was central to the larger liberal tradition because it anchored individual freedom in human nature.

Meanwhile, according to Meyer, the emerging traditionalist conservatives rightly understood the moral and political importance of virtue, and the role of family, faith, and community in inculcating it. However, they wrongly exalted the political claims of society over the individual, and foolishly ceded to government responsibility for overseeing virtue's transmission.

By correcting these mistakes, indeed by showing that each school supplied a vital insight needed to set the other straight, Meyer sought to establish that partisans of limited government and partisans of traditional morality were natural moral and political allies. Classical liberals could learn from the traditionalists that traditional morality provided the theoretical ground for the dignity of the individual, and that it took tight-knit families and vibrant communities to form rugged, self-reliant individuals. And traditionalists could learn from classical liberalism that to be of worth virtue must be exercised in freedom, and that government must be restrained so that families and communities—particularly religious communities—could mold morals and cultivate virtues. Classical liberalism, without traditionalism, could not explain why freedom was good, or provide for the sources that nourish freedom and the beliefs and practices that conserve it. Traditionalism without classical liberalism could not furnish an account of the principles of limited government most conducive to preserving family, faith, and community, and fostering virtue.

Among conservatives, Meyer's position came to be known as fusionism. This was unfortunate because it implied that classical liberalism and traditionalism could only be held together by a mysterious cosmic force. A better name for what Meyer espoused would be constitutional conservatism. It more accurately captures his grounding of conservatism in America's founding ideas, and the intellectual coherence of the alliance in American politics he forged between partisans of limited government and partisans of tradition.

Constitutional conservatism is also a good name for the views championed by Barry Goldwater, the longtime Arizona senator and modern American conservatism's first standard-bearer in national politics. As the 1964 Republican candidate for president, Goldwater ran as a passionate defender of individual freedom. He believed a passionate defense was needed because of the menace presented by what he regarded as the creeping socialism of an ever-expanding federal government and a Soviet communism that endured coexistence with the West but pursued total victory.

Goldwater's opponents successfully portrayed him as a reactionary who would undo the New Deal and a warmonger who would provoke nuclear conflagration—he lost to Lyndon Johnson in a landslide. Goldwater had tried to defuse the charge of extremism in his acceptance speech at the Republican National Convention in San Francisco with a defense of extremism, memorably concluding by proclaiming that "extremism in the defense of liberty is no vice" and "moderation in the pursuit of justice is no virtue."[16] Unfortunately, these rhetorical flourishes encouraged dangerous and persistent misconceptions among conservatism's critics as well as among conservatives themselves. Contrary to Goldwater's assertions, political moderation is a virtue crucial to the defense of liberty and to the pursuit of justice.

In fact, on the bigger question of the relationship between liberty and tradition, Goldwater counseled political moderation, or the recognition and reconciliation of competing constitutional imperatives. In his San Francisco acceptance speech, he declared his party's dedication to

> freedom made orderly for this nation by our constitutional government, freedom under a government limited by the laws of nature and nature's God, freedom balanced so that order lacking liberty will not become the slavery of the prison cell, balanced so that liberty lacking order will not become the license of the mob and of the jungle.[17]

---

16. Barry Goldwater, acceptance speech at the Republican National Convention, Cow Palace, San Francisco, July 16, 1964, available at http://www.national center.org/Goldwater.html.

17. Ibid.

This admonition to balance echoes the argument of his short 1960 book, *The Conscience of a Conservative,* which became a bestseller and set the stage for his 1964 candidacy.

In *The Conscience of a Conservative,* Goldwater maintained that "the day's overriding political challenge" was "*to preserve and extend freedom.*"[18] The pendulum had swung sharply in favor of government power, upsetting "the delicate balance that ideally exists between freedom and order."[19] To restore that delicate balance, it was necessary to recover the principle of limited government:

> The *legitimate* functions of government are actually conducive to freedom. Maintaining internal order, keeping foreign foes at bay, administering justice, removing obstacles to the free interchange of goods—the exercise of these powers makes it possible for men to follow their chosen pursuits with maximum freedom.[20]

Although there is abundant room for dispute over the legitimate functions, and their scope, to which Goldwater would have limited government, the devotion to limiting government to maximize freedom is a distinguishing mark of constitutional conservatism.

Progressive critics commonly contend that the conservative determination to limit government reflects a narrow, mechanistic, or economic view of man. To the contrary, Goldwater argued, true conservatism recognizes that man "is a spiritual creature with spiritual needs and spiritual desires," which "reflect the superior

---

18. Barry Goldwater, *The Conscience of a Conservative* (Miami, Fla.: BN Publishing, 2007, orig. 1960), p. 8.
19. Ibid.
20. Ibid., p. 11.

side of man's nature, and thus take precedence over his economic wants."[21] But what takes precedence morally and spiritually, according to Goldwater, must not take precedence for government. It is not government's function to directly cultivate and provide for man's moral and spiritual needs. The principal reason government must be limited to its proper functions is that its enormous powers pose a grave threat to the freedom without which man's spiritual needs and desires cannot be developed and satisfied. Keeping government within its proper limits gives families, religious communities, and voluntary associations the room they require to teach the moral virtues, and men and women the opportunities they need to exercise them. The moral virtues both reflect man's superior side and are essential to discharging well the many responsibilities that citizens in a free society shoulder at home, at work, and in civic life.

Despite grappling with the contending claims and mutual dependence of liberty and tradition, Goldwater was all but uncompromising in his repudiation of the welfare state. In the 1960s, moreover, staunch conservatives often resisted the use of the federal government to right the wrong of legally sanctioned racial discrimination. In both cases, conservatives sought to uphold the principle of limited government against vast expansions of the power of the federal government during a time in which the principle of limited government had few defenders among left-liberals and progressives. Although their judgment could be flawed and their rhetoric could veer to the apocalyptic, conservatives' muscular defense of limited government when the principle was subject to mockery and scorn made a crucial contribution to constitutional government in America. Nonetheless, conservative opposition to any and all expansion of government in

---

21. Ibid., pp. 4–5.

the 1960s tended to disregard real changes in people's sentiments and beliefs and real changes in the economy and society. It fell to those who came to be called neoconservatives—renegade scholars, thinkers, and policy makers who migrated from the left to the right—to seek to reconcile American conservatism to the welfare and regulatory state, and to the legitimate obligations of government to protect the equal rights of all.

The term "neoconservatism" was coined as a reproach by hostile critic Michael Harrington in 1973, and eventually embraced by Irving Kristol, first among neoconservatism's founding fathers, as a useful description of a genuine intellectual and political tendency or persuasion. In the mid-1960s, a small number of leading left-liberal intellectuals from the worlds of journalism and the academy—Daniel Bell, Nathan Glazer, Daniel Patrick Moynihan, Norman Podhoretz, and James Q. Wilson, among others—joined Kristol in criticizing the left-liberal political and intellectual establishment. At *The Public Interest*, which Kristol co-founded in 1965 and co-edited, at *Commentary* under Podhoretz's editorship, and on the op-ed pages of the *Wall Street Journal*, and elsewhere they exposed the overreach of Johnson administration Great Society welfare programs. They also vigorously defended bourgeois virtues against the vitriolic attacks of the late-1960s student movement and countercultural critics including more than a few professors, attacks that went beyond condemning this or that flawed American practice or policy to repudiating the very principles of American constitutional government and the American way of life. And they defended the traditional mission of the university to transmit knowledge and cultivate the mind against what they saw as rank politicization of the academy. For defending constitutional principles, bourgeois virtues, and liberal education, Kristol and company were denounced as apostates by the left-liberal establishment and sometimes as worse—neoconservatives.

Not all of those who were condemned as neoconservatives became conservatives. But by the 1990s, most had. By championing a form of conservatism that accepted the welfare and regulatory state as irreversible, salutary, and in need of aggressive limitation, neoconservatism encouraged libertarians and traditionalists to combat big government prudently, which meant applying principles in light, rather than in denial, of the realities of contemporary America.

In January 1976, Kristol sketched neoconservatism's defining features in an essay for *Newsweek,* "What is a 'Neoconservative'?"[22] He insisted that "it is only a tendency, not a clearly defined 'movement,' that there is much heterogeneity in it, and that to those who do not closely follow intellectual controversy in America, the term 'conservative' can be misleading." The term could be misleading because, in opposition to many conservatives of the time, neoconservatives generally approved of government provision of a social safety net to meet the changing needs of citizens in a "dynamic, urbanized society." At the same time, neoconservatism emphasized fiscal responsibility and "a minimum of bureaucratic intrusion in the individual's affairs," which earned neoconservatism conservative stripes. Neoconservatism, moreover, had "great respect—it is fair to say it has learned to have great respect—for the power of the market to respond efficiently to economic realities while preserving the maximum degree of individual freedom." To achieve "overriding social purposes," it preferred the provision of incentives to "direct bureaucratic control." It embraced equality of opportunity but rejected egalitarianism, or the quest to achieve through government regulation and redistribution "equality of

---

22. Irving Kristol, "What Is a 'Neoconservative'?," Rpt. in *The Neoconservative Persuasion: Selected Essays, 1942–2009,* ed. Gertrude Himmelfarb (New York: Basic Books, 2011), pp. 148–150.

condition for all citizens." No longer vainly opposing the welfare and regulatory state, neoconservatism sought to limit the welfare and regulatory state whose legitimacy it affirmed.

In addition, neoconservatives were "respectful of traditional values and institutions: religion, the family, the 'high culture' of western civilization." Neoconservatives did not deny that there was much in tradition that must be reformed and even discarded. Rather, they stressed that a misguided quest for unfettered freedom, particularly in matters of sex, had obscured the dependence of liberty on the wisdom stored in "the experience of generations." And in foreign policy, despite differences of opinion among its leading figures on major issues, including Vietnam, neoconservatives argued that promoting American principles abroad should be an American priority.

Twenty-seven years later, Kristol returned to the topic of neoconservatism's defining features in "The Neoconservative Persuasion," an essay that appeared in *The Weekly Standard,* edited by his son, William.[23] With the benefit of almost three decades of experience in the intellectual trenches, the elder Kristol could look back and proclaim that neoconservatism's "historical task and purpose" was "to convert the Republican Party, and American conservatism in general, against their respective wills, into a new kind of conservative politics suitable to governing a modern democracy."

In contrast to much of post–World War II American conservatism, which Kristol found to be often angry and mired in the past, neoconservatism had been "hopeful" and "forward-looking" and at ease with the idea that the state had a responsibility to pro-

---

23. Irving Kristol, "The Neoconservative Persuasion," Rpt. in *The Neoconservative Persuasion,* pp. 190–194.

tect the poor, the elderly, the sick, and the involuntarily out of work. But in contrast to the left, neoconservatives appreciated the formal limits on government's powers as well as the practical limits on its competence. In an up-to-date version of Burke's critique of the French revolutionaries, neoconservatives drew on empirical social science to deflate the pretensions, and systematically expose the often-disastrous consequences for the intended beneficiaries, of social engineering. They showed that the ambition, however well meaning, to cure society's ills through government planning and large-scale social projects routinely proceeded oblivious to or contemptuous of people's expressed interests, opinions, and sentiments. Instead of social engineering, neoconservatives championed economic growth because an expanding economy would form a "property-owning and tax-paying population" that would reject the "egalitarian illusions" fostered by policies that promoted expansion of government's reach and responsibilities.

Neoconservatives also emphasized democracy's dependence on culture and religious faith. Some were believers, some were uncertain but open to the claims of religious faith, and some were neither. But neoconservatives were generally friendly toward religion because they saw in the varied shapes it took in the United States a body of doctrines and a way of life that, by encouraging the discipline, devotion, and respect for human dignity that self-government presupposes, provided a corrective to the moral crudities of popular culture and its frequent message of untrammeled liberation.

In foreign policy, Kristol noted, neoconservatives stood for patriotism or love of country grounded in an appreciation of American principles and interests, particularly America's vital national security interest in defending democratic nations and promoting an international order dedicated to individual rights and political freedom. Neoconservatives opposed anything that smacked of world government because its inevitable lack of accountability and transparency would imperil freedom. And they counseled prudence in the conduct of diplomacy and war, which required distinguishing friends from enemies but had nothing to do with Carl Schmitt's antiliberalism[24] and everything to do with Burke's emphasis on experience in refining political judgment.

Notwithstanding its many-sidedness, neoconservatism in the last decade has come to be caricatured by elite opinion as a one-dimensional school of foreign policy devoted to the idea that the United States should aggressively use military might to promote democracy around the world. The caricature, which is not wholly unrelated to ideas championed by some neoconservatives and embraced by the George W. Bush administration, has all but blotted out the bigger picture. By embracing the welfare and regulatory state on the grounds that it was a necessary and legitimate response to changing times while seeking to restrain it in accordance with the principles of limited constitutional government as understood by *The Federalist,* and by affirming the need to balance liberty with tradition, order, and virtue as expounded by Burke, neoconservatism taught the centrality of the imperative to harmonize competing political principles—in other words, political moderation—to a viable contemporary conservatism.

Like social conservatives and libertarians, neoconservatives found a fitting standard-bearer in 1980 in Ronald Reagan. As was true of many neoconservatives, Reagan was for much of his adult life a Democrat, but his switch began earlier, with the renewal of American conservatism in the 1950s. His own political career was jump-started by "A Time for Choosing," a paid televised address he gave on behalf of Barry Goldwater's presidential campaign in

---

24. See Carl Schmitt, *The Concept of the Political,* Expanded Edition (Chicago: University of Chicago Press, 2007, orig. 1927).

October 1964, which wove together traditionalist and libertarian themes.[25] But Reagan dwelt on freedom. He explained that he had recently switched parties because Goldwater's Republican platform reflected the political principles and priorities to which he had long been committed but which the Democratic Party had abandoned: restrained federal spending; elimination of wasteful Washington bureaucracy and intrusive, ineffective, and counterproductive government programs; protection for the rights of private property; the return of power to states, local communities, and the people; and commitment not merely to containing but defeating communist totalitarianism, the great threat to freedom from abroad. His political principles and priorities, Reagan declared, reflected the founders' understanding of self-government as "the ultimate in individual freedom consistent with law and order."

Seventeen years later, at his January 1981 inauguration as the fortieth president of the United States, Reagan reaffirmed his commitment to limiting government to conserve freedom. With the nation confronting high inflation, high unemployment, high interest rates, high marginal tax rates, low productivity, and low growth, Reagan declared, in what would become one of his best known utterances, "In this present crisis, government is not the solution to our problem; government is the problem."[26] This broadside directed at the left was music to the ears of the right. But the problem presented by government in Reagan's judgment called not for a radical remedy but rather for robust reform. "The administration's objective," he went on to say, "will be a healthy,

---

25. Ronald Reagan, "A Time for Choosing," Oct. 27, 1964, available at http://www.reagan.utexas.edu/archives/reference/timechoosing.html.

26. Ronald Reagan, "First Inaugural Address," U.S. Capitol, Jan. 20, 1981, available at http://avalon.law.yale.edu/20th_century/reagan1.asp.

vigorous, growing economy that provides equal opportunities for all, with no barriers born of bigotry or discrimination." To deliver would involve not only cutting, curbing, and curtailing government but also redirecting government toward its proper goals: "Government can and must provide opportunity, not smother it; foster production, not stifle it." Indeed, by deploring "unnecessary and excessive growth of government," Reagan acknowledged the need—however carefully circumscribed—for necessary and appropriate government action. Although the connection between freedom and tradition or faith did not loom large in his inaugural address, Reagan thanked those who had attended the tens of thousands of prayer meetings held that day, and in passing he linked freedom and faith, declaring, "We are a nation under God, and I believe God intended for us to be free."

Two months later, in remarks to the Conservative Political Action Conference in Washington, D.C., President Reagan emphatically connected freedom and faith.[27] Describing Frank Meyer's achievement as "a vigorous new synthesis of traditional and libertarian thought" and commending it for capturing the spirit of modern conservatism, Reagan argued that limiting government, encouraging free markets, and honoring "the values of family, work, neighborhood, and religion" were not separate items but crucial elements of a single political agenda. In March 1983, addressing the annual convention of the National Association of Evangelicals in Orlando, Florida, Reagan again stressed the significance of Meyer's synthesis.[28] Declaring that liberty is a gift of God,

27. Ronald Reagan, "Remarks at the Conservative Political Action Conference Dinner," March 20, 1981, available at http://www.presidency.ucsb.edu/ws/index.php?pid=43580.

28. Ronald Reagan, "Remarks at the Annual Convention of the National Association of Evangelicals in Orlando, Florida," March 8, 1983, available at http://www.reagan.utexas.edu/archives/speeches/1983/30883b.htm.

Reagan maintained that it is not the state but "families, churches, neighborhoods, and communities" that foster the moral virtues on which liberty depends. And because it was devoted to recovering the ideas about the relationship between freedom and faith out of which America was formed, Reagan concluded, modern conservatism provided the best answer to America's political challenges.

On the domestic front, Reagan's signature achievement was the passage of the 1981 tax cut. He was so successful in making tax cuts the key to limiting government and expanding the economy that for going on three decades—and notwithstanding compromises on taxes later in his presidency—tax cutting has been the centerpiece of conservative orthodoxy. As Reagan biographer Steven Hayward pointed out, the Republican Party has followed Reagan's lead and more or less adopted Milton Friedman's belief that any tax cut at any time for any reason is good.[29] Reagan cut taxes over the objections of major figures in his party, including George H.W. Bush, who, before he became Reagan's running mate and while he was still contesting the 1980 GOP nomination, mocked Reagan's "voodoo economics." Likewise, Senator Bob Dole regarded tax cuts as irresponsible unless preceded, or at least accompanied, by spending cuts. Reagan prevailed by arguing that tax cuts not only encouraged economic efficiency but also promoted fundamental fairness. He succeeded in recasting the public debate about what government owes citizens from one that focused almost exclusively on entitlements, or obligations on the part of government to provide social and economic support, to one that stressed opportunities, or government's obligation to remove obstacles, particularly government-created ones, so that individu-

---

29. Steven F. Hayward, *The Age of Reagan: The Conservative Counterrevolution 1980–1989* (New York: Three Rivers Press, 2009), pp. 66–67.

als and the associations and organizations that they formed, could make their own way in the world.

Reagan won passage of substantial tax cuts in late July 1981. The top tax rate, starting with income on a joint return of $162,400, was cut by the largest percentage, from 70 percent to 50 percent. But sizable reductions were made down the line: "For a couple with $30,000 income, the rate fell from 37 percent to 28 percent; at $50,000, the rate fell from 49 percent to 38 percent. A household earning the median income of $22,000 in 1984 saved about $500 in taxes."[30] And notwithstanding the opprobrium progressive politicians and intellectuals heaped on the Reagan tax cuts, they inspired reductions in the taxation baseline around the world:

> In the ensuing years, nearly all industrialized nations would emulate the Reagan plan and reduce their marginal income tax rates. Even the Scandinavian social welfare states of Sweden, Norway, and Finland got in on the act. Norway cut its top tax rate from 75 percent to 54 percent, Finland cut rates from 71 percent to 54 percent, and Sweden from 83 percent to 75 percent. (Supply-siders suggest that Sweden's relatively poor economic performance relative to its neighbors is explained by the fact that it didn't cut its tax rates enough.)[31]

While it remains debatable under what circumstances and to what extent cutting taxes leads to equal or increased tax revenues and under what circumstances conservatives would be wise to compromise on taxes to secure cuts in spending, the evidence suggests that the Reagan tax cuts launched three decades of astonishing economic growth, amounting to the largest peacetime economic expansion in American history.

---

30. Ibid., p. 164.
31. Ibid.

A measure of how successfully Reagan changed the terms of the debate is that on the campaign trail in 2008, and as the most progressive of our presidents, Barack Obama has operated within a framework defined by Reagan's reform of the tax system. As candidate and president, Obama repeatedly promised no new taxes on individuals earning less than $200,000 and couples earning less than $250,000, and muted or disguised such tax increases as may be necessary to pay for the array of new entitlement spending he has enacted, starting with the individual mandate in the Affordable Care Act, which in June 2012 the Supreme Court found constitutional, but only as a tax.[32]

Meanwhile, Grover Norquist, president of Americans for Tax Reform, has won from almost all Republicans in Congress a pledge not to raise taxes—a pledge he won as well from 2012 Republican presidential nominee Mitt Romney and his running mate, Representative Paul Ryan. Refusing to contemplate a deal to offset spending cuts with tax increases might seem the antithesis of political moderation. And yet to counter the substantial increase in spending of the Bush years, followed by the enormous growth in government under the Obama administration, a determination to set a ceiling on taxes can be seen as an instrument of balance.[33]

Reagan's social policy also reflected a conservatism that simultaneously celebrated individual freedom and defended traditional morality. Consistently linking social-conservative goals to the protection of freedom, he opposed abortion, except in cases of rape or threats to the mother's health, because he believed that the unborn child, like all human beings, was endowed with unalienable rights

---

32. *National Federation of Independent Business et al. v. Sebelius, Secretary of Health and Human Services, et al.,* June 28, 2012, available at http://www.supremecourt.gov/opinions/11pdf/11-393c3a2.pdf.

33. See William Voegli, "Not a Penny More," *City Journal,* Winter 2012, available at http://www.city-journal.org/2012/22_1_taxes.html.

to life and liberty. And he supported a constitutional amendment to restore prayer in public schools because he believed religion nourished the spirit of liberty and should not enjoy less freedom than other forms of expression. Instructively, however, despite his opposition to abortion and support for school prayer, Reagan did not push either position aggressively, in part because he respected the political settlements the people reached on these divisive issues.

Reagan emphatically blended freedom and morals in foreign policy. Breaking with the realist school—exemplified by President Richard Nixon and his secretary of state, Henry Kissinger—which emphasized managing balances of power and minimizing the role of morality in strategic calculation, Reagan resolutely opposed Soviet communism not only because it represented a threat to American freedom but also because it cruelly subordinated the individual to the state. In the same March 1983 speech to evangelicals in which he declared liberty a gift of God, he also memorably branded the Soviet Union an "evil empire" for murdering tens of millions of its own citizens and using brutal force to expand its domains and condemn citizens of other nations to a blighted fate.[34]

Intellectual and political elites on the left were aghast. They still believed that Western liberal democracies had much to learn from Soviet communism about social justice. For their part, not a few on the right thought it was best for America to reduce its profile on the world stage and mind its own business.

Yet opposing communism, in part by promoting freedom, was central to Reagan's presidency. On June 8, 1982, he addressed members of the British Parliament and warned of "threats now to

---

34. Ronald Reagan, "Remarks at the Annual Convention of the National Association of Evangelicals in Orlando, Florida," March 8, 1983, available at http://www.reagan.utexas.edu/archives/speeches/1983/30883b.htm.

our freedom, indeed to our very existence, that other generations could never even have imagined."[35]

In identifying communism as the major threat from abroad, Reagan followed in the footsteps of President Harry S. Truman. On March 12, 1947, Truman had addressed a joint session of Congress to affirm his opposition to communist aggression. Communism was on the march, imposing totalitarian government throughout Eastern Europe; Greece and Turkey were tottering. The free world confronted a global struggle between "alternative ways of life."[36] To prevail in that struggle, Truman announced the doctrine to which his name became attached: "One of the primary objectives of the foreign policy of the United States is the creation of conditions in which we and other nations will be able to work out a way of life free from coercion." America would concentrate on creating the material conditions of freedom, which meant providing "economic and financial aid which is essential to economic stability and orderly political processes."

Similarly, Reagan warned at Westminster of the dire threat to freedom posed by "global war" in which the use of nuclear weapons "could mean, if not the extinction of mankind, then surely the end of civilization as we know it," as well as by the "the enormous power of the modern state" which, readily abused, worked "to stifle individual excellence and personal freedom." To defend freedom abroad, Reagan announced, American foreign policy would strive "to foster the infrastructure of democracy, the system of a free press, unions, political parties, universities, which allows a people to choose their own way to develop their own culture, to

---

35. Ronald Reagan, "Address to Members of the British Parliament," June 8, 1982, available at http://www.reagan.utexas.edu/archives/speeches/1982/60882a.htm.

36. Harry S. Truman, "Address before a Joint Session of Congress," March 12, 1947, available at http://avalon.law.yale.edu/20th_century/trudoc.asp.

reconcile their own differences through peaceful means." This mandate broadened Truman's understanding of the conditions under which freedom flourished and set a task Reagan recognized would "long outlive our own generation." Out of it was born the National Endowment for Democracy.

The moral dimension also figured significantly in Reagan's approach to arms control negotiations with the Soviets. In the early 1980s, he frightened and infuriated the left with his determination to rebuild the American military in general and, in particular, to counter the Soviet nuclear missiles targeting European capitals by deploying intermediate-range nuclear missiles in Europe. At the same time, Reagan declared his eagerness to meet with Soviet leaders to discuss not merely limiting the deployment of new nuclear weapons but actually reducing for the first time those that already existed.

Reagan's quest for arms reduction was driven by rejection of the dominant theory of deterrence. The theory of mutually assured destruction (MAD) held that a first strike with nuclear weapons could be prevented by the promise of a devastating retaliatory strike on the attacker's cities. Reagan considered this promise immoral. His alternative was the Strategic Defense Initiative (SDI), a program involving both ground- and spaced-based systems to defend the nation against incoming nuclear ballistic missiles. Progressives vehemently opposed the program, deriding it as technologically infeasible and strategically destabilizing. Yet SDI was more consistent with both classical just war theory and the modern laws of war than was MAD, whose essential feature was the targeting of tens of millions of civilians and vast expanses of civilian infrastructure.

Fear of American SDI technology and an inability to match the Reagan military build-up because of a frail economy helped persuade the Soviets to negotiate in earnest. In December 1987,

Reagan's approach bore fruit: The United States and the Soviet Union signed the Intermediate-Range Nuclear Forces treaty, agreeing for the first time to eliminate an entire class of nuclear weapons. By then, it would turn out, the Soviet Union's corrupt communist empire was on its last legs. Historians will continue to debate, but it is reasonable to conclude that Reagan's diplomacy, as well as the American economic boom, renovation of the military, support for dissidents in communist territory, and moral critique of the Soviet Union over which Reagan presided hastened the U.S.S.R.'s collapse and America's victory in the Cold War.

On the two greatest issues of his age, Reagan has been vindicated. He saw the need to limit the growth of the welfare and regulatory state to unleash innovation and energy, to make room for individual responsibility, and to allow family and faith to flourish. And he recognized that communism represented no mere rival but a cruel and unjust form of government, a sworn enemy of liberal democracy, and a profound menace to vital American national security interests, including a stable international order grounded in freedom and equality. In his quest to limit government and defeat communism, Reagan did not seek to fundamentally transform America or to return it to a golden past. Revolutionary as it may have seemed at the time to both critics and supporters, the so-called Reagan Revolution shifted directions, altered priorities, and recovered principles within a constitutional order and political culture that it inherited and left largely intact. Notwithstanding occasional extravagant rhetoric, Reagan accepted the New Deal principle that government had a fundamental role to play in providing a social safety net and kept in place a good bit of President Johnson's Great Society, while working to slow the rate at which government continued to grow. His presidency represents the high-water mark in modern American conservatism of the reconciliation of liberty with tradition, order, and virtue.

Attempting in the 1990s to follow in Reagan's footsteps, House Speaker and Georgia Representative Newt Gingrich promoted limited government, traditional morality, and strong national defense even as he fervently advocated sweeping change. Gingrich rose to prominence in 1994 by leading the charge against the transformative change that First Lady Hillary Rodham Clinton pursued as head of President Bill Clinton's task force on health care reform. The mid-term elections resulted in the first Republican majority in the House of Representatives in forty years and catapulted Gingrich to Speaker of the House. Gingrich and his fellow House Republicans had campaigned on ten legislative proposals they dubbed the Contract with America, which they promised to pass within the first hundred days of the new session of Congress. The Contract was not revolutionary. It aimed to make the federal government more efficient, transparent, and accountable, but did not seek to drastically alter relations between the federal government, state governments, and the people. Only four years after scaling the heights of congressional leadership, Gingrich was impelled to resign from the House in the face of ethics sanctions, embarrassing personal revelations, unpopular Republican efforts to remove President Clinton from office, and the GOP's loss of five seats in the 1998 mid-term elections.

Gingrich did enjoy notable accomplishments during his brief tenure as speaker, including the passage of many Contract with America provisions and the enactment of a major welfare reform bill signed by President Clinton in 1996. But rather than entrenching the conservative political realignment he envisaged, Gingrich left conservatism dazed and confused. One major cause was the grandiose pose he repeatedly struck as a revolutionary determined not merely to reform but to remake the American constitutional system by bringing to an end the era of big government and by re-injecting morals into American politics. Gingrich failed to appreciate the political moderation of the American people, who proved to be no more enamored of right-wing radicals than of left-wing radicals. He also failed to appreciate the political moderation of a constitutional conservatism, which respects the deliberation that the Constitution imposes on lawmakers, and which counsels reform that works with rather than rides roughshod over well-established practices and widely shared sensibilities.

In the 2000 presidential election, George W. Bush's advocacy of compassionate conservatism suggested that the Texas governor and his campaign architect, Karl Rove, had learned from Gingrich's rise and fall. Compassionate conservatism aimed to wed two convictions that did not obviously go together but that had strong roots in the American political tradition. The first conviction is often associated with the left but, as Bush correctly judged, it crossed party lines and ran deep in America at the turn of the twentieth century: government has a responsibility to assist the sick, the elderly, the involuntarily unemployed, and others who can not care for themselves. The second conviction, which Bush shared with his evangelical base and with neoconservative critics of social engineering, was that religious organizations often provide care that is better targeted and more effective than that delivered by government. By directing government support to faith-based relief organizations that agreed not to proselytize while delivering food, shelter, and health care, compassionate conservatism sought to balance liberty, morality, and faith.

The Bush administration's failure to make good on the promise of compassionate conservatism stems in part from the inherent difficulty of institutionalizing the right balance. But it is also due to the al-Qaeda attacks of September 11, 2001, which turned Bush into a wartime president less than eight months into his first term.

The Bush administration did not invade Iraq in March 2003 to spread democracy and freedom abroad but rather to enforce

17 U.N. Security Counsel Resolutions that over the course of more than a decade had obliged Saddam Hussein to account for, dismantle, and destroy Iraq's weapons of mass destruction and the programs that produced them, but which the Iraqi dictator had flagrantly defied. To be sure, Bush's democracy and freedom agenda was developed in the wake of the September 11 attacks but it only acquired prominence in his speeches in the fall of 2003 after the failure to find weapons of mass destruction in Iraq in the spring and summer of that year. The agenda wove together convictions thought to derive from antagonistic sensibilities. Like many national security hawks, Bush believed that the United States needed to take the battle to the Islamic extremists and the states that harbored and financed them. But much like progressives and liberal internationalists with roots extending back to Woodrow Wilson, Bush also believed that the United States advanced its vital national security interests by using diplomacy, financial assistance, development expertise and, where necessary, the military, to promote liberty and democracy abroad.

On Nov. 6, 2003, President Bush addressed the United States Chamber of Commerce in Washington, D.C., at an event honoring the National Endowment for Democracy's twentieth anniversary.[37] Carrying forward the tradition of the Truman Doctrine and the principles Reagan expounded at Westminster, Bush's speech marked the first time a U.S. president focused the democracy and freedom agenda on the Muslim Middle East. Like Truman and Reagan, Bush looked beyond the moment to the long term. Securing and extending freedom in the Middle East, he declared,

---

37. George W. Bush, "Remarks by President George W. Bush at the 20th Anniversary of the National Endowment for Democracy," United States Chamber of Commerce, Washington, D.C., Nov. 6, 2003, available at http://www.ned .org/node/658.

must be "a focus of American policy for decades to come." The universal claims of human freedom did not dictate a single set of political institutions, but all democracies that protect freedom must conform to certain "vital principles." They must "limit the power of the state"; establish the "consistent and impartial rule of law"; "allow room for healthy civic institutions—for political parties and labor unions and independent newspapers and broadcast media"; "guarantee religious liberty"; "privatize their economies, and secure the rights of property"; "prohibit and punish official corruption, and invest in the health and education of their people"; "recognize the rights of women"; and they must, "instead of directing hatred and resentment against others . . . appeal to the hopes of their own people."

The ambiguous results the United States achieved in Iraq and Afghanistan under President Bush—and the convulsions during President Obama's watch that have marked the Arab Spring in Egypt, Libya, Syria, and elsewhere—do not undermine the democracy and freedom agenda. However, they do demonstrate that cultivating the conditions under which freedom flourishes abroad can only be the arduous, gradual, patient work of generations. And because the democracy and freedom agenda requires weaving together vital principles and translating them into practice in diverse and remote settings, it depends on political moderation to the highest degree.

Bush's most distinctive domestic policy initiative and foreign policy commitment reflected a determination to balance competing moral and political imperatives. Nevertheless, conservatives were demoralized by a litany of Bush administration shortcomings: soaring domestic spending; unforced errors in developing a legal regime for the novel challenges presented by Islamic terrorism; the botched reconstruction of Iraq; the GOP's decisive electoral losses in 2006 and 2008; and the eruption of a far-reaching economic crisis at the end of his second term.

Uncertain of the principles that should bind them as Bush left office, social conservatives and libertarians seemed inclined to turn inward and go their separate ways. President Obama and his progressive ambitions have done much to reenergize conservatives and renew their common sense of purpose and urgency. His slim victory over Mitt Romney in November 2012 showed that much work is still to be done. Constitutional conservatism well understood helps explain why conserving the liberty that social conservatives and libertarians both rightly prize depends on renewing the appreciation and cultivation of political moderation.

CHAPTER 5

A Way Forward

It is a misfortune, inseparable from human affairs, that public
measures are rarely investigated with that spirit of moderation
which is essential to a just estimate of their real tendency to advance
or obstruct the public good; and that this spirit is more apt to be
diminished than promoted by those occasions which require an
unusual exercise of it.

—James Madison, *The Federalist,* No. 37

In the four great causes that marked his career—America,
Ireland, India, and the French Revolution—Edmund Burke
sought to conserve the conditions under which liberty flourished
and correct bad policies and flawed laws that violated liberty's
requirements. In seeking to bring British politics in line with liberty's conditions and requirements, he exposed the error of
depending on abstract theory for guidance in practical affairs. He
taught the supremacy in political life of prudence, or the judgment
born of experience, bound up with circumstances, and bred in
action. He maintained that good policy and laws must be fitted to
the people's morals, sentiments, and opinions. He demonstrated
that in politics the imperfections of human nature must be taken
into account and the nongovernmental institutions that cultivate
the virtues must be respected. And he showed that political moderation frequently counsels rejecting the path of least resistance

and is sometimes exercised in defending principle against majority opinion.

Burke's words and example are as pertinent in our time as they were in his own. Today's conservatives should heed them as they come to grips with two entrenched realities that pose genuine challenges to liberty and whose prudent management is critical to the nation's well-being.

The first entrenched reality is that the era of big government is here to stay. This is particularly important for libertarians to absorb. Over the last two hundred years, society and the economy in advanced industrial nations have undergone dramatic transformations. And for three-quarters of a century, the New Deal settlement has been reshaping Americans' expectations about the nation-state's reach and role. Consequently, the U.S. federal government will continue to provide a social safety net, regulate the economy, and shoulder a substantial share of responsibility for safeguarding the social and economic bases of political equality. All signs are that a large majority of Americans will want it to continue to do so. While conservatives must redouble their efforts to reform sloppy and incompetent government and resist government's inherent expansionist tendencies and progressivism's reflexive leveling proclivities, the attempt to dismantle or even substantially roll back the welfare and regulatory state reflects a distinctly unconservative refusal to ground political goals in political realities. Conservatives should focus on restraining spending, reducing regulation, reforming the tax code, and generally reining in our sprawling federal government. But they should retire misleading talk of *small* government. Instead, they should think and speak in terms of *limited* government.

The second entrenched reality, this one testing social conservatives, is the sexual revolution, perhaps the greatest social revolution in human history. The invention, and popularization in the mid-1960s, of the birth control pill—a cheap, convenient, and effective way to prevent pregnancy—meant that for the first time in human history, women could reliably control reproduction without abstinence. This greatly enhanced their ability to enter the workforce and pursue careers. It also transformed romance, reshaped the structure of the family, and refashioned marriage. Brides may still wed in virginal white, bride and groom may still promise to love and cherish for better or for worse until death do them part, and one or more children may still lie in the future for many married couples. Nevertheless, ninety percent of Americans engage in premarital sex; cohabitation before marriage is common; childbirth out of wedlock is increasingly routine; divorce, while emotionally searing, is no longer unusual, legally difficult, or socially stigmatizing; children, once the core reason for getting married, have become optional; and civil unions for gays and lesbians have acquired majority support, while same-sex marriage is not far behind.

These profoundly transformed circumstances do not oblige social conservatives to alter their fundamental convictions. Social conservatives should continue to make the case for the traditional understanding of marriage with children at the center, both for its intrinsic human rewards and for the benefits a married father and mother bring to rearing children. And they should back family-friendly public policy and seek, within the democratic process, to persuade fellow citizens to adopt socially conservative views and vote for candidates devoted to them. But given the enormous changes over the last fifty years in American sexual mores and family organization—and with a view to the enduring imperatives of limited government—they should refrain from attempting to use the federal government to enforce the traditional understanding of sex, marriage, and the family. Social conservatives can remain true to their principles even as they adjust their expectations of what can be achieved through democratic politics and renew their appreciation of the limits that American constitutional government imposes on regulating citizens' private lives.

Some conservatives worry that giving any ground—sometimes in regard to the welfare and regulatory state, sometimes in regard to the sexual revolution, sometimes in regard to both—is tantamount to sanctifying a progressive status quo. But that is to mistake a danger for a destiny. Seeing circumstances as they are is a precondition for preserving one's principles and effectively translating them into viable reforms. Even under the shadow of big government and in the wake of the sexual revolution, libertarians and social conservatives, consistent with their most deeply held beliefs, can affirm the dignity of the person, the inseparability of human dignity from individual freedom and self-government, the dependence of individual freedom and self-government on a thriving civil society, and the paramount importance the Constitution places on maintaining a political framework that secures liberty by limiting government.

Confusion persists in many quarters about what a return to the Constitution entails. Some hard-driving conservatives see such an undertaking as an opportunity to restore simplicity and purity to American politics. Influential progressive politicians and pundits have tried to portray a return to the Constitution as a reactionary grasping after an imagined past. Both opinions are at odds with the balancing and blending at the heart of a constitutional conservatism—at least a constitutional conservatism that takes its bearings by Burke, *The Federalist,* and the high points of post–World War II American conservatism.

Constitutional conservatism well understood grounds a return to the Constitution in the devotion to individual liberty and limited government that united the Constitution's framers and their Anti-Federalist opponents. It appreciates the tensions that inform the Constitution and which are intrinsic to the task of preserving liberty: government's powers must be ample and energetic but restrained; grounded in interest but elevated by virtue; and based on the consent of the governed while aimed at securing rights not subject to majority whim or will. And it stresses that balancing worthy but conflicting political principles depends on cultivating the spirit of political moderation institutionalized by the Constitution.

Political moderation, as I have argued, is a constitutional imperative and a demanding virtue. Although it is often disparaged as a mask for spinelessness or a cloak for soullessness, the imposter should not be confused with the real thing. Political moderation doesn't mean selling out causes or making a principle of pragmatism. It does not mechanically direct one to the middle of the road, nor does it command or consecrate bipartisanship. It is, as Burke's political courage makes manifest, consistent with taking strong stands and opposing popular movements even as circumstances may well dictate the opposite. Political moderation recognizes with Burke that "all government, indeed every human benefit and enjoyment, every virtue, and every prudent act, is founded on compromise and barter."[1] At the same time, political moderation refuses, as did Burke, to sanctify compromise and barter as ends in themselves. They are valuable for their capacity to vindicate principle on the most favorable terms that circumstances permit.

Constitutional conservatism well understood does not mandate particular policies or command specific laws, but it does bring into focus the overarching aims and larger considerations that, in

---

1. Edmund Burke, "Speech on Conciliation with the Colonies," *The Works of the Right Honourable Edmund Burke,* Vol. II (London: John C. Nimmo, 1887), p. 169, available at http://www.gutenberg.org/files/15198/15198-h /15198-h.htm#CONCILIATION_WITH_THE_COLONIES.

a free society, should inform policy and underlie law. It insists that federal laws and government programs involve a legitimate exercise of a constitutionally-grounded government power. It emphasizes that government initiatives and actions must promote and not weaken self-reliance, personal responsibility, industriousness, innovation, thrift, and the other virtues of liberty. It supports government undertakings that invigorate families, neighborhoods, voluntary associations, and religious communities while opposing government undertakings that enervate them. And it seeks to reduce the tasks performed by the federal government that, although in the federal purview, would confer greater public benefits if performed by more local forms of government, civil society, or the private sector.

Constitutional conservatism well understood endorses progress. It takes inspiration from the people's intentions, proclaimed in the Constitution's preamble, "to form a more perfect Union, establish Justice, insure domestic Tranquility, provide for the common defence, promote the general Welfare, and secure the Blessings of Liberty to ourselves and our Posterity." It takes to heart that the protection of individual freedom unleashes curiosity, experimentation, and risk-taking, all of which naturally foster an interest in improvement, including improvement in the quality of government. And it appreciates that it will often have something to learn from left-liberals and progressives, both because political issues tend to be complex and many-sided and because in some matters left-liberals and progressives may well be better attuned to the nation's needs.

To be sure, not all forms of progress are equally consistent with the spirit of political moderation in which the Constitution was conceived. Constitutional conservatism well understood vigorously opposes interpretations of progress that bring bigger, bossier, more brazen government dictating an ever-expanding array of rules and regulations to achieve increasingly uniform outcomes; that unleash unsustainable government spending which strangles the economy and dims all citizens' prospects for a decent future; and that, by shifting responsibilities from individuals and the private sector to government, foster a culture of dependency that transforms self-reliance and success into vices and victimhood into a virtue.

Constitutional conservatism well understood enthusiastically embraces progress conceived as the improvement of the laws to better protect individual freedom, promote economic prosperity, and fortify individual responsibility. It proudly affirms, as does Representative Paul Ryan's "Roadmap for America's Future," that the federal government has justly acquired over the last century, and can discharge consistent with constitutional principles, a duty to provide a social safety net for the sick, the elderly, the very young, and those who through no fault of their own are unable to find work.[2] And it recognizes that since capitalism, which is inseparable from liberty and self-government, can corrode the virtues that sustain freedom, government must impose reasonable regulations on commerce, and must not harm—and, where possible given its limited means, should foster—the nongovernmental associations that sustain the virtues of freedom.

Constitutional conservatism well understood provides a framework for developing a distinctive political agenda to which both social conservatives and libertarian conservatives can subscribe in good conscience. At its broadest, it will embrace a domestic policy that energetically pursues fiscally sound, market-based, growth-oriented solutions to put people back to work, pay down the debt, and reform health care, social security, the tax code, and energy and environmental regulation. At the same time, and recognizing that liberty and democracy depend on culture but also limit government's authority and ability to cultivate hearts and

---

2. "A Roadmap for America's Future," Plan 2.0, available at http://roadmap.republicans.budget.house.gov/plan.

minds, constitutional conservatism demands that the government vigorously protect First Amendment speech rights while encouraging government to promote in the private sphere and civil society the humanities and fine arts.

A constitutional conservatism will pursue a defense policy that maintains American military preeminence because it is indispensable to America's interest in and responsibility for safeguarding an international order that favors freedom. It will also devote substantial resources to protecting the nation against new and emerging threats of mega-terror in a manner that is as committed to individual liberty as it is to national security, and is prepared, in light of constitutional principles, to responsibly fashion the inevitable painful tradeoffs.

And it will craft a foreign policy that is grounded in justified pride in America and the rights of national sovereignty. In the spirit of the Truman Doctrine, the Reagan Doctrine, and the Bush Doctrine, it will reaffirm America's vital national security interest in advancing liberty and democracy abroad while realistically calibrating missions—military, diplomatic, and developmental—to the nation's limited knowledge and finite resources. It will promote free trade; seek opportunities to advance human rights; respect international law and institutions while opposing the excesses to which they are increasingly subject; and form alliances and operate multilaterally as much as possible but will be prepared to act alone, particularly where vital national security interests are at stake.

The priorities of a constitutional conservatism will change with changing circumstances. In the near term, it will seek at home to reduce the number of abortions and increase the number of adoptions. It will work to keep the question of same-sex marriage out of the federal courts and subject to consideration by each state's democratic process. It will combat illegal immigration in a manner that is emphatically pro–border security and pro–lawful immigrant. It will promote school choice, particularly in our inner cities where public schools have failed most grievously, because school choice gives low-income parents the opportunity to place their children in classrooms where they can obtain a decent education, and it enhances individual freedom and encourages competition. It will restore liberal education at our public universities and set a standard for private universities and colleges by vigorously protecting liberty of thought and discussion; promoting intellectual diversity as the most urgently needed form of diversity in higher education; and eliminating federal regulations that compel universities to adopt sexual misconduct regulations, grievance procedures, and disciplinary boards that strip the accused of due process protections indispensable to the dignity of the individual. And it will support the appointment of judges who recognize that their duty is to interpret the Constitution and not to legislate; who understand that the Constitution created a limited government with enumerated powers whose overriding purpose was to protect individual liberty; and who, where the Constitution is most reticent, discern the strongest obligation to uphold the results of the democratic process.

None of these broad policies and priorities is unfamiliar. Embracing them as a whole that flows from the determination to combine liberty with the claims of tradition, order, and virtue will challenge both social conservatives and libertarians.

Indeed, honoring the imperatives of a constitutional conservatism will require both social conservatives and libertarians to bite their fair share of bullets as they translate principles, priorities, and policies into concrete legislative programs, national security measures, and diplomatic initiatives. But they will work from a position of strength as they accommodate, balance, and calibrate in behalf of the individual freedom on which the highest hopes of both depend. That strength derives from the lesson of political moderation inscribed in constitutional conservatism well understood.

Acknowledgments

The main arguments of this book are stronger and suppler for having been exposed to trenchant criticism from my colleagues on Hoover's Boyd and Jill Smith Task Force on Virtues of a Free Society, which I had the pleasure of cochairing with Hoover Institution Deputy Director David Brady. We are both indebted to the Smiths and to Hoover Institution Director John Raisian, who worked with the Smiths to provide task force members generous support for the study of the principles and practices that underlie the American constitutional order.

Much appreciated also has been the backing of the William E. Simon Foundation's Jim Piereson and Bill Simon, both themselves students of liberal democracy in America and the virtues on which it depends.

For going on ten years, Tad Taube and the Koret Foundation of which he is president have played an indispensable role in enabling me to research and write about, among other things, American political ideas and institutions. I am delighted to have this occasion to thank them.

I am grateful to former *Wall Street Journal* editorial features editor Robert Pollock, *Wall Street Journal* deputy editorial features editor Howard Dickman, *Real Clear Politics* Washington editor Carl Cannon, *PJ Media* CEO Roger Simon, *National Review*

Online editor-at-large Kathryn Jean Lopez, and Hoover colleague and *Policy Review* editor Tod Lindberg for providing excellent opportunities to develop my ideas in their pages and pixels. As a young assistant professor in the Department of Government at Harvard University, I was fortunate to learn from my then–senior colleague Harvey C. Mansfield—now, happily, also a Hoover colleague—to appreciate "America's constitutional soul." Throughout the course of this project, Ethics and Public Policy Senior Fellow Stanley Kurtz and Tel Aviv University Professor of Political Science Azar Gat provided much-appreciated encouragement. Harvard Law Professor Jack Goldsmith, also a colleague on Hoover's Koret-Taube Task Force on National Security and Law, read several chapters and offered astute advice. Hoover colleague Emily Messner furnished vital research and editorial assistance, and served as an ever-sensible sounding board for hunches and hypotheses. And in the course of proofreading the book, my sister Linda Berkowitz ferreted out lingering errors.

In recent years, I have had the opportunity to teach American political thought to talented students abroad—at Underwood International College at Yonsei University in Seoul, South Korea; and in Israel at the Argov Fellows program and the Tikvah IDC program at the Interdisciplinary Center, Herzliya, and at the Tikvah Jerusalem summer institute at Hebrew University. I have always found teaching rewarding. This time around it has been a special pleasure and highly instructive to observe the salience of the principles of American constitutional government to young friends of freedom in faraway places.

About the Author

PETER BERKOWITZ is the Tad and Dianne Taube Senior Fellow at the Hoover Institution, Stanford University, where he cochairs the Jill and Boyd Smith Task Force on Virtues of a Free Society and chairs the Koret-Taube Task Force on National Security and Law.

He studies and writes about, among other things, constitutional government, conservatism and progressivism, liberal education, national security and law, and Middle East politics.

He is the author of *Israel and the Struggle over the International Laws of War* (Hoover Institution Press, 2012), *Virtue and the Making of Modern Liberalism* (Princeton University Press, 1999), and *Nietzsche: The Ethics of an Immoralist* (Harvard University Press, 1995).

He is the editor of *The Future of American Intelligence* (Hoover Institution Press, 2005); *Terrorism, the Laws of War, and the Constitution: Debating the Enemy Combatant Cases* (Hoover Institution Press, 2005); the companion volumes *Varieties of Conservatism in America* (Hoover Institution Press, 2004) and *Varieties of Progressivism in America* (Hoover Institution Press, 2004); and *Never a Matter of Indifference: Sustaining Virtue in a Free Republic* (Hoover Institution Press, 2003).

In 2004, with co-editor Tod Lindberg, he launched Hoover Studies in Politics, Economics, and Society, a series of concise books on leading issues and controversies.

He has written hundreds of essays, articles, and reviews on many subjects for a variety of publications, including the *American Political Science Review*, the *Atlantic*, the *Boston Globe*, the *Chronicle of Higher Education*, *Commentary*, *Haaretz*, the *Jerusalem Post*, the *London Review of Books*, *National Review*, *The New Republic*, the *New York Post*, the *New York Sun*, *Policy Review*, *The Public Interest*, *Real Clear Politics*, the *Times Literary Supplement*, the *Wall Street Journal*, the *Washington Post*, *The Weekly Standard*, the *Wilson Quarterly*, and the *Yale Law Journal*.

He holds a JD and a PhD in political science from Yale University; an MA in philosophy from the Hebrew University of Jerusalem; and a BA in English literature from Swarthmore College.

About the Hoover Institution's
BOYD AND JILL SMITH TASK FORCE
ON VIRTUES OF A FREE SOCIETY

THE BOYD AND JILL SMITH TASK FORCE ON VIRTUES OF A FREE SOCIETY examines the philosophical foundations, historical development, and implications for contemporary public policy of the virtues on which liberty in America depends. The philosophical, historical, and public policy inquiries are tightly connected. Only by recovering America's founding principles and charting the changing beliefs and practices of American moral and political life can we understand the forces that today endanger the virtues that sustain freedom and meet the challenge of preserving the associations—particularly families, religious communities, and schools—that cultivate those virtues.

The members of this task force are Peter Berkowitz (cochair), David Brady (cochair), Gerard V. Bradley, James W. Ceaser, William Damon, Robert P. George, Tod Lindberg, Harvey C. Mansfield, Russell Muirhead, Clifford Orwin, and Diana Schaub.

Books published by members of, and contributors to, the
BOYD AND JILL SMITH TASK FORCE ON VIRTUES OF A FREE SOCIETY

*Constitutional Conservatism: Liberty, Self-Government,
and Political Moderation*
Peter Berkowitz
HOOVER INSTITUTION PRESS, 2013

Endangered Virtues
Edited by Peter Berkowitz
ONLINE VOLUME, HOOVER INSTITUTION, 2011
http://www.hoover.org/taskforces/virtues/endangered-virtues

Conserving Liberty
Mark Blitz
HOOVER INSTITUTION PRESS, 2011

Designing a Polity: America's Constitution in Theory and Practice
James W. Ceaser
ROWMAN AND LITTLEFIELD, 2011

*Failing Liberty 101: How We Are Leaving Young Americans
Unprepared for Citizenship in a Free Society*
William Damon
HOOVER INSTITUTION PRESS, 2011

What So Proudly We Hail: The American Soul in Story, Speech, and Song
Amy A. Kass, Leon R. Kass, and Diana Schaub
INTERCOLLEGIATE STUDIES INSTITUTE, 2011

Alexis de Tocqueville: A Very Short Introduction
Harvey C. Mansfield
OXFORD UNIVERSITY PRESS, 2011

Index